It has well been said that prayer can do anything that God can do. I am grateful for John Franklin's wonderful book, *And the Place Was Shaken*. As a pastor for many years, I have struggled with the subject of leading powerful prayer meetings. This book will be an asset to pastors such as I, and Christian leaders everywhere. I am happy to commend it.

Adrian Rogers, Pastor Emeritus
Bellevue Baptist Church, Cordova, Tennessee

I know of no one better than this author to speak to the subject of prayer. He not only is capable of writing on this ministry, but he has been very effective in leading our prayer ministry here at Woodstock's First Baptist Church. You will be challenged and instructed in this excellent book.

Johnny Hunt, Pastor
First Baptist Church, Woodstock, Georgia

I cannot imagine a more timely and urgently needed resource. This tool has a wonderful balance of biblical principle and practical application. Best of all, it is God-focused and brings churches to the Savior, not just a program format. I wholeheartedly recommend this book to every leader with any responsibility for guiding prayer!

Gregory Frizzell
Prayer & Spiritual Awakening Specialist
Baptist General Convention of Oklahoma

John Franklin's contribution to the growing prayer movement in North America is exceptional. Biblical united prayer toward the Kingdom is one of the most critical prayer mobilization issues facing the church today. *And the Place Was Shaken* not only challenges leaders to take seriously the call to lead God's people toward corporate prayer, it provides practical tools for appropriate action. The blending of the "why" with the "how to" creates a ripe environment for God's Spirit to equip, inspire and speak. A job well done!

J. Chris Schofield
Senior Consultant, Office of Prayer Evangelism Strategy
Baptist State Convention of North Carolina

AND
THE
PLACE
WAS
SHAKEN

AND THE PLACE WAS SHAKEN

HOW TO LEAD A POWERFUL PRAYER MEETING

JOHN FRANKLIN

BROADMAN
&HOLMAN
PUBLISHERS

NASHVILLE, TENNESSEE

Ten-Digit ISBN: 0–8054–3298–1
Thirteen-Digit ISBN: 978–0–8054–3298–5

Published by Broadman & Holman Publishers
Nashville, Tennessee

Dewey Decimal Classification: 264.7
Subject Heading: PRAYER MEETINGS

Scripture is quoted from the New King James Version,
copyright © 1979, 1980, 1982,
Thomas Nelson, Inc., Publishers.

1 2 3 4 5 6 7 8 9 10   10 09 08 07 06 05

Contents

Preface

This is a book for those who lead prayer meetings. It is not a general book about prayer. I am supposing that you, as a prayer leader, already know how to pray and understand the principles of prayer. You know that prayer cannot be manipulated or regimented, but you also recognize that prayer meetings have their own very practical problems. You want to be an instrument in God's hand that leads his people to experience his manifold presence as they gather before the throne of grace.

Let's overview the eight chapters of the book. Chapter 1 establishes the nonnegotiable mandate for corporate prayer by looking at God's working in Bible times, in the ages following, and in our own day. Many churches today have quit having prayer meetings because the meetings were flat and hardly anyone came. In this chapter you will find that the case for praying together is so strong that you won't give up if people don't respond immediately.

Chapter 2 explains why some prayer meetings are dead and others are dynamic. Before Orville and Wilbur Wright could fly, they had to unlock the secrets of flight. To watch a bird fly was one thing. To know the aero-dynamics at play was another. If you have ever been in a dynamic prayer meeting, you know when God is present, but you may have difficulty identifying why God is working. This chapter lists six keys to dynamic prayer meetings.

Chapter 3 is the core of the book. You will discover the three things that God wants to do in a prayer meeting and your four responsibilities as a prayer leader to work with God to fulfill them. God's three desires are to reveal himself to his people, to move his people onto his agenda, and to minister to his people, especially through his people. The leader's four responsibilities are to design a God-centered format; to employ activities that involve the heart, mind, and body of the people; to shepherd God's people; and to discern God's activity. You will find all these principles in Solomon's temple dedication service. Then you will use a one-page work-sheet to design your own prayer meeting.

Chapters 4, 5, 6, and 7 explore in depth the four responsibilities outlined in chapter 3. Chapter 4 proposes a God-centered format—focusing on God, leading his people to respond from their hearts, seeking first the kingdom, praying for personal needs, and closing in celebration. Chapter 5 gives you activities that involve people at the heart, mind, and physical level. This includes bulleted lists of some down-to-earth things you can do in working with God. Chapter 6 explores how to shepherd people in a prayer meeting. Jesus taught people the relationship with the Father, moved people onto God's agenda, ministered to their needs, and spoke to their heart for transformation. Ways to do this are listed. Chapter 7 discusses how you must discern God's activity in order to work with him. Listed are examples of God's activity before, during, and after the prayer meeting that will help you know how to recognize and respond to God.

Chapter 8 recognizes that you live in the real world, with real people. Many times obstacles exist such as fear of praying out loud, resistance to change, or just plain apathy. This chapter makes suggestions for transitioning a prayer meeting until people know how to function in God's presence.

I am deeply grateful to many who have impacted my life, resulting in the writing of this book. First, and foremost, I thank our glorious Lord and Savior, Jesus Christ, who loved me and gave himself up for me to redeem me from my sin—even while I was his enemy. Every good thing that has ever happened in my life was initiated by him. Next, I thank my parents who raised me in the knowledge and fear of the Lord as a child, and have continued to be one of my greatest sources of encouragement even to this day. Between 1989 to 1991 God opened my understanding to the importance and basic principles of corporate prayer through seminary friends, and of those none more so than Pamela Robinson. Moreover, I have been deeply influenced by two godly men—T. W. Hunt and Henry Blackaby—both of whom have prayed for me and helped me understand much about the Lord. Henry Webb at LifeWay became the catalyst for this book being written. Unbeknownst to me he initiated contacts at Broadman & Holman that resulted in a request for a manuscript. Finally, during the writing process a wonderful team of intercessors prayed for me. My expression of thanks to these cannot even begin to adequately convey the debt I owe to each of them. I only pray that whatever kingdom good results from this book will go to their credit, and that my Lord will be glorified through my inadequate efforts. He alone is worthy!

Finally, we desperately need revival in our day. Knowledge of how to seek God's face corporately has dimmed in most churches and has even been extinguished in some. My prayer for this book is that it will help you bring God's people back to him. In writing that last statement, I recognize the absolute inability and inadequacy I gave this work to produce that result. I might just as well try to bind up the wind. If you are blessed in any way through reading this book, then may the glory go to God, to whom it is due.

John Franklin

CHAPTER 1

The Priority of Praying Together

In June 1990 I found myself unexpectedly in awe. I had joined a team of about 250 people to participate in a two-week evangelistic crusade in Mombasa, Kenya, a seaside city of roughly a million people. The organizers divided most of us into teams of three, and we went hut to hut, house to house, presenting the gospel. There is no other way to describe those fourteen days except that the glory of God simply descended: nearly thirty thousand people responded to the gospel. A few times in my life I have been in a service or prayer meeting where the manifest presence of God could be felt but never before in a whole city. Wherever we walked, the presence of the Lord tangibly permeated the land, so much so that often people were being saved by the dozens. I could tell many stories to illustrate just how amazing the experience was, but one in particular captures it.

Our team of three had just finished witnessing in one of the villages, and we were walking down a dirt road that led to the next village. Up ahead were several Kenyan men seated on stools by the roadside. As we approached, one of them arose, walked briskly toward us, and greeted us in English. (This was not totally unusual because Kenya had been a British colony.) "Excuse me, are you from America?" he asked with an obvious agenda.

"Yes."

He continued, "Are you one of the ones who has come here to tell us the word of God?"

Again I answered, "Yes."

His voice intensified solemnly. "We've heard that you've come, and we've heard of Jesus and his great power. Tell me, how does one become his follower? My friends and I want to know."

I explained the plan of salvation, and without the least trace of hesitation, he immediately replied, "Let's pray."

I thought, *That was too easy. He must not have understood.* So I explained it again.

"I understood the first time," he said impatiently. "Let's pray!"

Do you see why this story sums it up? The glory of God fell so powerfully that people came to us to be saved.

You've picked up this book about how to lead prayer meetings, and that's a nice little story I just told. What have they got to do with each other? Actually, everything.

The revival in Mombasa had begun months earlier through prayer meetings, and prayer meetings had continued steadily until our arrival. In fact, during our two-week stay a different church prayed all night each night. I had been learning that God requires prayer as a prerequisite to his working powerfully, so I prayed I could attend one of these meetings. God in his graciousness promptly answered, and a few days later I found myself in an all-night prayer meeting. Four congregations had come together to pray in one of the churches.

That church, one of the nicest I saw, was by our standards a crude structure with sparse accommodations. The floor was rough, unfinished concrete. Homemade benches of plank lumber served as pews. Two or three low-watt lightbulbs provided all the lighting. Open windows allowed a little air flow, the only air-conditioning. Most American garages are nicer than this building. However, in stark contrast to this humble building stood the rich hearts of the people. Faces etched in joy fervently worshipped the Lord. They sang, testified, listened to preaching, and prayed. We disbanded, and I went to bed at 7:00 a.m. Four hours later I awoke totally refreshed without the least trace of fatigue. So great was the presence of God in my hotel room that I didn't even rise from my bed. I slid out from under the sheets to my knees. Through Bible reading I sensed that our day would be particularly blessed, and that's exactly what happened. That afternoon in our witnessing, not a single adult rejected the gospel, the only day that happened.

Do you see the connection? The whole revival had come through prayer meetings, and the greatest day I experienced followed an all-night prayer meeting.

This chapter has one purpose, but it's not to convince you that we must pray if we would see the power of God. You might assume that based on the experiences I've just shared, but I have something much more specific in mind. Before I tell you what it is, I want to stress the significance of what you're about to read.

Imagine us at a coffee shop sipping drinks and chatting about spiritual concerns. When the topic turned to prayer, you would see me preface this truth by putting down the cup and pushing it aside, leaning forward with eyes narrowed, and speaking in a lowered voice. "What I'm about to tell you is one of the reasons most churches don't have much spiritual power. Churches today have generally abandoned this practice." You would catch the intensity and conviction in my tone: *The greatest workings of God come by corporate prayer, and we will not see the power of God in sufficient measure to transform the world around us until we pray together. As a leader you must make praying together a priority equal to preaching and teaching.*

If I sound a little melodramatic, good. Then you caught just how monstrously important it is. I want to sow this seed of conviction in your heart so that when you complete this chapter, you will conclude that your spiritual fate depends not just on prayer but on praying in community with other Christians. Personal prayer lives alone will not result in the working of God to the degree needed for spiritual transformation in our lives, our churches, our cities, or our nation. God in his sovereignty has determined that something happens when we pray together that transcends praying separately. His working increases exponentially. I am not trying to minimize the role of our personal prayer life. In fact, I believe that private and corporate prayer are like two wings of an airplane. Which one would you rather do without? The absence of either would be fatal. If we don't pray together, we will continue losing our country. If we do pray together God's way, we can expect a revolution of our society.

The Reasons This Is True

What's the hard-core evidence to support these statements? Many exist, but we'll focus on five proofs. I'm listing them in the order I learned them.

1. What the Apostles Believed and Practiced

Have you ever been reading the Bible when something happened to you? You suddenly realized that a passage you had been reading all your life does not mean what you thought it meant? Let me tell you how it happened to me early one morning several years ago. I opened my Bible to Acts 6, my quiet time passage for the day. To be candid I approached it halfheartedly. I knew that chapter recorded what many call the choosing of the first deacons. To give it a little spice, I flipped open the Greek on my Bible software. I began reading in verse 1: "Now in those days, when the number of the disciples was multiplying, there arose a complaint against the Hebrews by the Hellenists, because their widows were neglected in the daily distribution."

The word *distribution* was actually *diakonia* in Greek. It's from the same basic root family as the word *deacon* and *ministry*. It wasn't just a functional duty; you could see the ministry aspect of serving people. *How interesting,* I thought, *but no big deal.*

I continued reading verse 2: "Then the twelve summoned the multitude of the disciples and said, 'It is not desirable that we should leave the word of God and serve tables.'"

The word *serve* was *diakonein* in Greek—the same root family. But again, *no big deal.*

I read on in verse 3: "Therefore, brethren, seek out from among you seven men of good reputation, full of the Holy Spirit and wisdom, whom we may appoint over this business."

Then I came to verse 4, and it happened! I was riveted with the truth of this passage. In English it reads:

"But we will give ourselves continually to prayer and to the ministry of the word."

That's not what it says in Greek. It literally reads, "But we to the prayer and the *diakonia* of the word will steadfastly continue." When I read that, I pushed away from the computer screen in disbelief.

All my life I had interpreted that passage to mean the apostles recognized the need to delegate ministry responsibilities to others so that they would be freed up to spend time in prayer and receive a fresh word from the Lord to preach to the people. They realized they couldn't become so enmeshed in the work of the Lord that their personal relationship with him suffered and therefore become ineffectual from the pulpit (or wherever they preached/taught in the first century). I always assumed they were referring to their personal prayer life.

Perhaps I concluded that from experience. Right out of seminary I assumed the helm of a church with only three members left. Only one faithful family remained, and as a young twenty-five-year-old, I went there to rebuild the broken foundations with them. I discovered an interesting dynamic. I quickly realized I not only had the honor of preaching the sermon on Sunday but also of scrubbing the toilet on Monday. Any work to be done fell to one of us four. Soon in the bustle of activity, my own personal prayer time suffered, and I found a negative effect on my preaching. Not having as much time in prayer hurt my sensitivity to God's voice, and I felt the effect in my preaching. This experience colored my belief that the apostles modeled the need to delegate responsibilities in order to guard time for prayer to preach powerfully.

That morning in my quiet time I realized that was not the point of this passage. The apostles were not referring to their personal prayer life but to the ministry of mobilizing the people of God to pray together. They were declaring that the two ministries they especially must do as church leaders were mobilizing the church to pray and preaching/teaching the Word of God. Do you see why I was so amazed? The implications were tremendous!

Here's the clues that led to my conclusions that the passage speaks of the ministry of prayer instead of their personal prayer lives. First, the context of the passage revolves around ministries. Verse 1 reveals a problem with a ministry. In verse 2 the apostles discuss what ministry they will and won't do. In verses 3–4 they choose to put seven men in charge of the ministry to widows while they focus on prayer and the ministry of the word. I could almost see them drawing this up on a chalkboard like a football coach. "OK team, the *O*s will take the widows; the *X*s will take prayer and the Word. Any questions?" Nothing in this passage refers to anything personal, only ministries.

Second, although the word *ministry* does not specifically occur before the word *prayer*, the definite article *the* does. The verse reads, "But we to the prayer and the diakonia of the word will steadfastly continue." They do not mean prayer in general; rather they have something specific in mind. The syntax creates the possibility that prayer and the word are twin ideas. Later I read thirteen commentaries to double check. Eleven of them didn't comment either way, but the two that did confirmed a reference to corporate prayer.

My surprise soon turned into a squirming discomfort because of the implications. I mused, *Are the apostles actually saying that out of all the ministries they could do, what they cannot let go of is preaching/teaching the Word of God and leading the prayer life of the church? Is this really what the Bible pictures here—that leaders ought to consider guiding the corporate prayer life of the church just as critical a priority as preaching/teaching the Word of God?* I thought, *I'd better be right on this one. I'd better not draw such a weighty conclusion from one passage alone.* Then an idea popped into my mind. *If this is indeed the case, then it should be reflected in the book of Acts. The apostles should live their lives that way.*

I looked up every occurrence of prayer in Acts preceding chapter 6 and discovered prayer mentioned five times: Acts 1:14, 24; 2:42; 3:1; 4:23–31. Amazingly, every verse pictured the apostles leading others in prayer; not once is their personal prayer life recorded. In every instance we see the apostles involved in leading the people of God to pray together. These stories confirm that Acts 6:4 speaks of a corporate ministry of prayer.

This pattern certainly strengthened the case, but I wanted to be sure. Then I thought, *If the apostles really believed this way, where would they have gotten that idea?*

The obvious answer is Jesus. I decided to study Jesus' prayer life and what he taught about prayer.

2. What Jesus Modeled and Taught on Prayer

I searched the words *pray, prays, prayed, praying, prayer, prayers, ask, asks, asked, asking, watch, watches, watched,* and *watching* in my concordance. I used seven criteria for selecting verses (see Appendix A), but basically I was after Jesus' teaching on prayer. I wanted to know what he commanded or gave as a condition for God to answer favorably. I identified thirty-seven verses in the Gospels that fit these criteria and discovered an amazing reality. Out of those thirty-seven verses, the word *you* was plural in thirty-three of the thirty-seven verses. *You* can be either singular or plural in English, but there is a difference in the Greek. Given the individualistic nature of American society, most people tend to read it as singular even when the opposite is true. For example, Matthew 7:7 and Mark 11:25 actually say:

You all ask, and it will be given to you all;
you all seek, and you will all find; you all knock,
and it will be opened to you all.

And whenever you all stand praying, if you
all have anything against anyone, you all forgive
him, that your Father in heaven may forgive all
of your trespasses.

The fact that Jesus taught in the corporate made a compelling case by itself, but Jesus also framed the condition for answered prayer in such a way that heightened the stipulation of praying together. He told his disciples in Matthew 18:19, "Again I say to you that if two of you agree on earth concerning anything that they ask, it will be done for them by My Father in heaven." He could have said, "If anyone asks . . . ." Instead he deliberately crafted his words in the plural. Evidently God has designed prayer to require that we pray together.

Most of Jesus' recorded times of private prayer occur prior to his choosing his disciples (Mark 1:37; Luke 3:21; 6:12), whereas after choosing them, most of his recorded prayer times involved the disciples (Luke 9:28; 11:1; Matt. 26:40). Even in the garden of Gethsemane, when facing the greatest crisis of his life, the looming shadow of the cross, he asked the disciples to watch with him. In every way, he modeled and commanded the need to pray together.

The case was growing for corporate prayer, but I still wanted to test this truth in other ways. Knowing that God is the same yesterday, today, and forever, I decided to look at the pattern of the Bible as a whole. Another surprising dynamic emerged.

3. The Pattern of Scripture Before and After the Resurrection

I sought to answer this question: Did the mighty moves of God come primarily through the prayer life of an individual or two or more believers? To find the answer, I read Genesis through Esther, then Acts through

Revelation. Throughout both the Old and the New Testaments are examples of private and corporate prayer, and God exercised his power through both examples. However, it quickly became apparent that a defining moment, a spiritual watershed, divided the way God worked. In the Old Testament God usually chose an individual through whom to exercise his power in response to prayer. For example, God only spoke with Abraham about the promised son (Gen. 15:4). Moses was by himself on Mount Sinai interceding for the people when God decided to forgive them (Exod. 32:14). Joshua by himself apparently cried out for the sun to stand still (Josh. 10:12). No one other than Samson pleaded to God for the temple to come tumbling down (Judg. 16:28).

Of course, corporate prayer does exist in the Old Testament, such as the temple dedication and revivals; but even then it is exercised in a markedly different manner from the New Testament. Typically the pattern in the Old Testament is that the people cry out to God, but the answer does not come to anyone except the judge or the prophet (twice the prophetess, perhaps directly to the king on occasion). Most often kings seem dependent on hearing from the prophet (1 Kings 22:8; 2 Sam. 24:7; 1 Chron. 12:5; 2 Chron. 11:2; 12:7; Isa. 38:2–5). Likewise, the people of God consulted the man of God (1 Sam. 9:9) because they did not hear for themselves. God usually did not answer them directly but primarily answered them through a prophet, an intermediary.

In the New Testament this radically changes. In the book of Acts, the 120 are gathered in an upper room praying in one accord when Pentecost comes (Acts 1:13; 2:1). The group prayed for wisdom in knowing who Judas's replacement should be (Acts 1:24). When Peter and John reported the Sanhedrin's threats, the church cried out to God in one accord for boldness, and the place was shaken (Acts 4:24, 31). They prayed over the seven chosen to serve the widows (Acts 6:6). Peter and John interceded for those who had not received the Holy Spirit yet, and he came (Acts 8:15–17).

Peter was in prison, but the church was fervently pleading with God for him (Acts 12:5). While the prophets and teachers were praying and fasting, the Holy Spirit called Paul and Barnabas to go on their first missionary journey (Acts 13:1–2). Then the church prayed before sending them out (Acts 13:3). Paul and Barnabas commended the new churches to God by prayer (Acts 14:23). Paul and his companions were going to prayer when Paul cast the demon out of a slave girl (Acts 16:16). Paul and Silas were praying when the earthquake happened that resulted in the jailer's conversion and their release (Acts 16:25). Paul prayed with all the Ephesians in his farewell address (Acts 20:36). Finally, they prayed with the disciples from Tyre (Acts 21:5).

Again, the goal is not to deny the role of individual prayer. Ananias was praying alone when he was told to go to Saul (Acts 9:10). Peter was alone on the rooftop when he had his famous vision leading him to Cornelius

(Acts 10:9). However, in Acts and in the rest of the New Testament, the majority of God's recorded workings came when his people prayed together.

This transition naturally raised the question, Why the difference from the Old to the New Testament? No verse expressly spells it out, but I believe it's safe to make logical conclusions based on the covenant change. Under the Old Covenant the people of God conducted their relationship with God through the law. Because the veil was not yet rent, they did not have access to God in the same way we do today. In the Old Testament, when God wanted to speak to his people, no one except the prophets or a few leaders could directly interact with God. This is why God's response to individual prayer dominates in the Old Testament. That radically changed under the New Covenant. Hebrews 8:11 states, "None of them shall teach his neighbor, and none his brother, saying, 'Know the LORD,' for all shall know Me, from the least of them to the greatest of them." Now his Holy Spirit has been poured out on all believers (Acts 2:17). Every child of God has equal access to the throne of God.

The fact that every Christian can know God experientially creates the possibility for believers to experience God together; however, the possibility alone means little. We could all be like millions of radios all receiving transmissions from a single tower but still individual, separate, stand-alone units. But Scripture teaches that the moment God saves us, we are baptized by the Holy Spirit into one body (1 Cor. 12:13). The foundation of our new spiritual life requires interdependence. Of course, interdependence does exist in the Old Testament but not in the same sense. The analogy of a body is not used for the people of God until after the birth of the church. The baptism into the Holy Spirit so intricately joined us together that we are no longer independent units fitted together; rather we are like flesh and sinew. God so raised the level of connectivity that just as a body part can't accomplish its function except by depending on other body parts, neither can we do much of spiritual significance except when we are connected and inter-dependent with one another.

Although our roles and functions vary, God does not allow us to conduct our personal relationship with him in isolation. He has ordained that our service in Christ requires teamwork with others. This does not mean a believer's personal prayer life is now obsolete or has become of lesser importance, but it does imply that being a body mandates that we regularly encounter him together. Focusing on the personal prayer life only would be equivalent to trying to play Mozart with one hand. All ten fingers are absolutely needed to create the music. Likewise, the body life of the New Covenant spills over into every aspect of our relationship with God and with others, demanding that we practice both per-sonal and corporate prayer.

The scriptural evidence proved convincing, but I also decided to test history. If that's the way God worked in the Bible, then he also should be consistent throughout the ages. I applied the same basic question: Since the resurrection, when have the greatest moves of God primarily occurred?

4. The Evidence of Prayer in God's Great Works

A study of church history and conversations with experts confirmed my expectations. In fact, I did not discover a single example in which the church transformed the culture when Christians did not spend significant time praying together. Here are a few examples.

In 1857 America was in the middle of a strong economy. As is so often the case in times of prosperity, morals began to slip, and interest in the things of God decreased. Alarmed by the spiritual state of affairs, a Dutch Reformed layman named Jeremiah Lamphier tacked up notices in New York City calling for a weekly prayer meeting on Wednesdays from noon till one. The first week only six people came, and none of them arrived before 12:30. The next week, though, the attendance jumped to twenty. Then the numbers nearly doubled again, and on the fifteenth day they began meeting every weekday to pray. About that time Wall Street crashed. The ensuing financial panic arrested the country's attention and turned hearts toward heavenly matters. So great and so immediate were the changes that in less than six months' time ten to fifty thousand businessmen were meeting daily in New York to pray during the noon hour. Inexplicably, that little, inauspicious prayer meeting Lamphier called became the pattern God used. By 1858 the movement leaped to every major city in America. The response of God to his people was that a million Americans out of a population of thirty million were converted in less than two years. At the height of revival, perhaps fifty thousand a week were being saved. These examples indicate that the working of God in history is consistent with the biblical pattern.

Fervent prayer meetings precipitated the Shantung Revival in northern China between 1927 and 1937. God's Spirit suddenly descended, and the once-anemic church ensconced in a spiritually dead culture began witnessing with dramatic results. One Chinese pastor commented, "When this revival began, we had about fifty members in our little church. Now we have at least one Christian in each of the one thousand homes in this town." Another pastor repeated a similar experience. His little church had only thirty members, but when the revival came, he baptized eighty-nine on one occasion, 203 on another occasion, and twenty to thirty every month after that. No one knows with certainty the number of conversions, but given the testimony of Dr. C. L. Culpepper, one may logically deduce that hundreds of thousands were brought into the kingdom—perhaps as many as one million.

The activity of God in answer to corporate prayer may also be seen on a smaller scale. Rees Howells journeyed to South Africa as a missionary. Six weeks after arriving, he joined in a prayer meeting. Out of that came an outpouring of the Holy Spirit in which they had two revival meetings a day for fifteen months and all day on Friday. Thousands were converted as a result.

J. O. Fraser, a missionary to the Lisu people in southwest China, saw tens of thousands of conversions during his ministry. He encouraged small-group prayer in England for his ministry.

Hudson Taylor, the great missionary to China, called a prayer meeting to ask for one hundred new missionaries. He then returned to England and spoke to a large group. One hundred men and women volunteered to return with him, and $55,000 in cash was donated, even though he had not asked for a single offering.

The same pattern is evident throughout history. I then applied this test to God's activity today.

5. Corporate Prayer and God's Mighty Works Today

Let me ask you a question: "How's Christianity doing on a worldwide scale? Are we winning or losing?" If the Lord tarries, future generations will probably look back on ours with envy. Christianity is dramatically advancing across the world.

The most optimistic scenario I've heard came from Avery Willis, vice president of the International Mission Board. He reported in the fall of 1999 that it is possible that 70 percent of all people who have ever been saved have come to Christ in the twentieth century—70 percent of that number since 1945, and 70 percent of the conversions post-1945 conversions since 1990. That means that at the turn of the twenty-first century, possibly one-third of all Christians who have ever lived have been converted since 1990! In Nepal just two thousand Christians were known in 1990, but ten years later that number had grown to half a million. Cambodia claimed only six hundred Christians in 1990 but reported sixty thousand by the beginning of the twenty-first century. Mozambique had no known Christians in 1988, and now three hundred churches exist in just one area. Just a few years ago in Asia, there were about fifteen million Christians; today there are more than 100 million. In Korea during the twentieth century the country advanced from being about 2 percent Christians to perhaps 40 percent Christian today.

The African continent has about the same percentages, with East Africa especially ranking as one of the greatest movements of God in history. I've already mentioned my story out of Kenya, but other African countries are also experiencing the hand of God. Uganda, for example, once suffered terrible atrocities under the Islamic dictator, Idi Amin, who ravaged the country. Later the number of people with HIV/AIDS skyrocketed to claim approximately one-third of the population. So devastating was the crisis that the World Health Organization predicted the collapse of the Ugandan economy by the year 2000. Today revival has come to that country, and the AIDS rate is down to 5 percent. So great is God's working that one church alone went from seven to two thousand in attendance in two weeks;

currently they have twenty-two thousand members and have planted 150 other churches.

In our hemisphere about forty thousand evangelicals lived in South America; today there are about forty million. Central America likewise is experiencing a tremendous movement of God. In India one denomination tracked about three million conversions in eight years. Even the Muslim world, although not experiencing the same kind of large numbers, has also seen an astronomical increase in converts.

Christianity is advancing in most quarters except four primary areas. If you live in North America, you know one of them. The other three are Japan, Australia, and Western Europe. Guess what one of the common denominators is everywhere Christianity marches forward? The Christians spend significant time praying *together.* In Korea and China many churches meet every morning to pray at least an hour before going to work, and then they have all-night prayer meetings on Friday. In India the believers began prayer meetings once or twice each week for their lost neighbors. In all the areas of the world where Christianity is growing, Christians spend time praying together.

In America we still practice the ministry of the Word. It's a centerpiece in most Protestant worship services. Outstanding radio teachers can be heard anywhere in the country. Christian books, videos, CDs, and tapes proliferate. Many churches have Bible study groups and Sunday schools. However, by and large we have abandoned meaningful prayer meetings. Most that remain are anemic and weak. This begs the question: might there be a connection, especially in light of God's activity worldwide? Could we be spiritually imploding because we've forsaken what the apostles guarded as one of their top two priorities?

Do you see why I've written this chapter? These modern-day examples of God's working reflect the biblical and historical pattern that we must pray together if we are to see God's power in sufficient measure. By and large American Christians have abandoned fervent, united, corporate prayer. The apostles, Jesus, the pattern of Scripture, history, and God's current working today bear witness that until we return to this practice we should expect to see continuing decline in societal morals and an increase in powerless churches.

If you are a leader of the people of God, you must make your ministry of mobilizing the people of God to pray together an equal priority with preaching and teaching the Word of God.

Why Is Praying Together So Important?

We must pray together, but why? *Why* has God ordained that we must pray together? Why were the apostles so adamant that they couldn't give up the ministry of corporate prayer? After much consideration I finally understood.

1. The Heart Stays in a Love Relationship.

I used to think that the reason the early church had such power with God was because they practiced missions and evangelism. From experience I had observed that whenever a church aggressively involved itself in missions and evangelism, God blessed that church. That should be no real surprise, for Jesus commanded some form of the Great Commission on at least four different occasions after his resurrection. So naturally I assumed the *cause* of their power with God in Acts stemmed from their obedience to be on mission with him.

I no longer believe that. I now believe their practice of missions and evangelism was the *effect* of their power with God. Here's why I say that: have you ever tried to lead someone to practice missions and evangelism who does not spend any time in the Word of God or regularly cry out to God with other believers? It's closely akin to pulling teeth. What do you have to do to motivate that person? Everything you know to do, and even then it rarely works. But let me ask you another question. What do you have to do to involve a believer who is spending regular time devouring, applying, and obeying the Word of God, who is constantly on his knees with other dynamic believers, crying out to God and experiencing God move in response to his prayers? Far from beating him into action, you merely have to point out the opportunity.

Do you see what the apostles were thinking as leaders? They assumed, "If we can do the two things that have the most immediate, direct, heart impact on those we lead; if we can guide them to apply the Word and encounter the presence of God with other believers, then most of the work of the church will naturally follow." The effect of the apostles practicing the two ministries that most immediately and directly impacted the heart was that the people served God in evangelism and missions. The by-product of hearing and obeying the Word of God and praying with others was being on mission.

I'm not advocating we do nothing to encourage missions and evangelism, but I am saying the emphasis of leading should fall on shepherding God's people. If the heart's soil is fertilized, the stalk of service quickly sprouts. Isn't it interesting that in most American denominations conversions have flatlined or declined in the midst of a tremendous population growth and an increasing number of evangelism programs? In my own denomination we are baptizing no more than we were fifty years ago. There used to be a one-to-twenty ratio of baptisms to members. Now it's over one to forty. We've doubled in size, but our churches are producing an inferior quality of believer. Not coincidentally we began abandoning the sanctity of our midweek prayer service in the 1950s and filling up that time with competing programs. Some churches have abandoned the prayer meeting altogether; others keep some leftover form of it, but in reality it is nothing more than another service with token attention given to prayer. And the prayers offered are usually nothing more than an organ recital—lungs, livers, kidneys, hearts. The heart has been denied the presence of God, and the love relationship has withered.

2. The People of God Stay on His Agenda.

The book of Acts records seven crises that threatened to derail the church from God's agenda, but the church successfully handled them. These accounts follow a fourfold pattern.

1. The church is growing.
2. Trouble arises that threatens the church's continued effectiveness.
3. The people resolve the problem successfully.
4. The church prospers.

For example, Peter and John are threatened to stop proclaiming Jesus but correctly respond to the intimidation (4:17, 33). Ananias and Sapphira violate the holiness of the church, but Peter quickly deals with it (5:9, 14). The apostles are arrested and beaten, but they continue proclaiming the Word (5:40, 42–6:1). The widow conflict poses a potential church split, but the people resolve it (6:1–7). Persecution arises at the stoning of Stephen, but the apostles persist in preaching (8:1, 4). Herod kills James and slates Peter for execution, but God releases him (12:2–11). Certain Jews teach that Gentiles must be circumcised to be saved, but the apostles refute that error and avert a church split (15:1, 22, 32).

Luke explicitly recorded corporate prayer in resolving two of these threats to God's agenda, and it exists in another story. When the Sanhedrin threatened Peter and John, God gave them the boldness they needed through praying together (4:31). Peter escaped Herod's clutches because the church interceded for him (12:5). In resolving the ministry to widows, they prayed over the seven they appointed. Although other stories do not have prayer listed explicitly, we can confidently assume prayer played an integral role. Acts 2:42 and 6:4 reveal it was a lifestyle practice of the leaders and people, so they naturally would have spent time in prayer even when it was not recorded in other stories.

Because they depended on God, they never were sidetracked in their mission. Neither external threats nor internal conflict derailed the church. They continued in one accord, and from the strength of that position, the church turned the world upside down. The ear of their heart stayed tuned to the voice of God's heart. The howling winds of persecution, the troubled waters of differences of opinion, and the land mines of faulty theological belief systems did not overcome that glorious group. Guiding the people of God to stay in the presence of God guarded their usefulness to God.

3. You Model What You Want Others to Practice.

What is important to those you lead, and what do they practice? They will do what they see you practice.

God gave you your assignment to guide others spiritually. People by nature are imitators. It's much easier to grasp something by watching and participating than by simply reading and discussing it. I learned this afresh through cohosting a conference with First Baptist Church, Woodstock, Georgia. In seven months they went from about one hundred in prayer meeting attendance to as many as one thousand, and God was answering prayer powerfully. When this happened, we decided to hold a conference on having a dynamic midweek prayer service and promote it throughout multiple states. The one-day event consisted of training from 9:00 to 4:15, followed by actually participating in the church's prayer meeting that evening.

To my surprise more than six hundred attended, about half of them pastors. Hearts were obviously stirred, so much so the energy was palpable, and the evaluations bore witness to how positively conferees viewed their experience. However, the real evidence came over the next fifteen months. I've been in many services with spiritual spasms—excitement for three days, then back to normal—nothing more than transitory emotional interruption. However, I received unsolicited feedback from attendees fourteen of the next fifteen months about what a difference the conference had made in their churches when they implemented the principles they learned. The fruit remained from this conference. In every instance except one, the comments were along these lines: "The teaching times were good, but what really helped me was actually experiencing the prayer meeting that evening." If you want to teach others to pray, you must model prayer.

The apostles knew the best discipleship strategy was to model prayer and create opportunities to pray.

Conclusion

Do you see why leading your church to grow in praying together is so important? By leading other believers to pray, you will engage in one of the most important practices of the Christian life. You will encourage those you lead to stay in a love relationship with God; you will create an infinitely greater likelihood that you stay on God's agenda; and you will practice the means through which God has chosen to work. If we are to see a spiritual awakening in this land, a reversal of the headlong rush into the moral cesspool in which we currently swim, then there must be fervent, intense prayer meetings sprouting up all over this land. If your church would see the power of God in supernatural ways, if the power of God is to descend so that Christians are renewed and the lost come under conviction of sin, then you must lead your people to pray. I know of no other foundation equal in importance to praying together, save repentance and the Word. May God bless you as you seek to follow him more fully in this matter.

CHAPTER 2

What Makes a Prayer Meeting Dynamic?

A friend asked me, "If the average church were to cancel its prayer meeting, would it make any significant difference in the spiritual life of the church or its effectiveness in the world?" Integrity demands that his candid question grapple with the statistical facts bearing witness to the spiritual anemia plaguing our current meetings.

Consider the evidence. On this generation's watch we have witnessed the speediest, greatest moral collapse in our nation's history. Over the last forty years illegitimate births have increased over 300 percent; crime has risen exponentially; marriage has become an endangered institution with one out of every two ending in failure. The homosexual agenda succeeds rapidly; promiscuity spreads incalculably. The content of television and a host of other societal ills bear witness that this nation is morally imploding before our watching eyes. If we have been praying, then that certainly hasn't stopped it, much less turned the tide. How odd that Jesus said the gates of hell shall not prevail against the church, yet on every hand evil prevails. How odd this happened in a nation founded substantively on Christian principles, replete with a heritage influenced by Christians. How odd that a godless minority backed only by the power of the devil could defeat a supposed Christian majority claiming to be backed by the power of God!

Worse yet, the spiritual anemia fares no better among Christians. In surveys done by Barna in 1997, he polled attitudes, beliefs, opinions, and lifestyles of those who claimed to be Christian and those who did not. In fifty-nine of sixty-six categories, there was no significant statistical difference between the two. Six years later in 2003, the situation proved no better. A survey released November 3, 2003, revealed that 49 percent of born-again Christians believed living together before marriage was morally acceptable, while 35 percent affirmed as acceptable having a sexual relationship with a member of the opposite sex who was not a marriage partner. Membership has been in massive decline in many denominations. Church splits, scandals, and a host of sins have proliferated until they're assumed to be common.

If God really does answer prayer, if there really is power in prayer, then we had better snap out of denial mode and look at the evidence. Every indication points to only one of two conclusions: *Either he's not really God, or our prayer meetings have not secured his power on our behalf.* Either his arm is shortened, or he must be trying to get our attention. Of course, you know the right answer. But why has God stayed his hand? Why does he look on without acting as the enemy comes in like a flood? What is it about our prayer meetings that allows him to remain silent at such a time as this? These facts don't just communicate; they scream that something's wrong.

So what's wrong? And more importantly, how would you go about changing it? Several times in my Christian experience I have been to a conference or read a book that motivated me to change and gave ideas and prescriptions for effecting that change. I tried to implement some of the ideas, only to fail. After some time I realized why. The ideas either assumed or didn't know certain foundations were in place. They were giving me the building materials of drywall, carpet, paint, light fixtures, and doors but were missing (or I didn't listen) the fundamentals of concrete slab, frames, and decking. The reason it was so hard to pick up on what was going on is that the visible external materials were exciting. When building a new house, do homeowners spend extensive time trying to decide what type of foundation they want? Do they ask about color variations in the concrete or which type of pine to use for studs? Instead, their energies are spent deciding on countertops, cabinets, flooring, and wallpaper. Often it's tempting to focus solely on the externals of colors and styles because they create the sense of home—warmth, mood, and life. A piece of wood is, well, just a piece of wood.

There's a second reason for ignoring foundations. When you look at finished houses, *you can't see them.* You *see* the externals. When you look at a successful church, the visible will be their attendance, programs, activities, buildings, Web site, and other attractive elements. But these externals work only when they're built on solid foundations. The same is true of prayer meetings. The churches I have known intimately with dynamic prayer meetings had internals in place. When I think back over the prayer meetings I have led, some were dead and some were dynamic. Not once can I think of a time that the foundations weren't in place in the dynamic ones.

I don't want to write a book with just the glowing testimonies of what God has done without telling the context in which he did it. That can lead to frustration when he doesn't do it where you are. You can't build a house with carpet; you can only lay the carpet to make the house more functional or attractive. Doors create privacy, but I wouldn't expect them to support trusses. No one would want to live in a house without these additions, but you only add them if the foundation is first in place.

I will give you some external building materials in chapters 4–6, but I want to spare you the ignominy of doing the right things that don't work. Understanding the truths I'm about to share helped me understand why I have led prayer meetings that were dead or dynamic while using the same format and activities.

Foundation 1
God-Centered Relationship

Throughout the Bible and history, the sheer weight of numbers never determined some critical mass needed to tip the hand of God. No, often the course of human events was altered by just a few. The Pentecost prayer meeting boasted a mere 120 attendees, Peter's release from prison stemmed from the cries of a little house church, and the great missionary journeys of Paul were launched by a handful of just five prayer warriors. No, God does not look at the tally sheet as if X amount of human power is necessary to help carry him over the hump. Instead he looks for a certain dynamic, a spiritual reality in the hearts and minds of those praying. God stayed or stirred himself up based on this one reality especially. The solution, therefore, to connect with God is to finger the sticking point that moves his hand.

What is the sticking point? Probably no example in the Bible better illustrates it than the track record of the apostles. Have you ever compared their before and after performance from the Gospels to Acts? In Matthew,

Mark, Luke, and John, their requests include calling fire down from heaven, sending people away hungry, and sitting on the right and left—just to name a few. Their actions fare no better, demonstrating continual lack of faith, stopping someone from casting out demons, and prohibiting children from coming to Jesus. Occasionally they get it right, but most of the time they are in left field while Jesus is in right. Consequently, Jesus rarely did what they asked. To be sure, their relationship with him remained, but they weren't transformation agents of their society.

Turning to the book of Acts, look again at their track record. Here we read that God used them to turn the world upside down. Acts records no account that they ever failed in their faith again. When God looked on their prayer meetings, three thousand were converted in a single day, the place where they prayed was shaken, and prison doors swung open. What a drastic contrast! Obviously some glorious transformation, some radical change, some revolutionary dynamic had occurred. What was it? What made the difference?

If we would see the transformation of our prayer meetings, we must line up with Acts. If you lead a prayer meeting small or large, everything hinges on whether you know the key. The first secret that unlocked the resources of heaven for them was this: they went from being on their own agenda to being on God's agenda. They quit seeking a seat on Jesus' right and his left and began praying for boldness to testify in the face of persecution. They quit flirting with a return to fishing and focused on shepherding the people of God. They stopped worrying about their circumstances and began seeking an endowment of power from on high to preach the gospel. *They changed from being self-centered to being God-centered.* This determined their power with God— or rather God's power through them.

And that's the way it's always been throughout Scripture when God moved mightily in answer to prayer. Consider other significant responses to prayer. What were the dynamics? Why did Elijah believe God would actually drop fire from heaven on a water-soaked sacrifice? What made Jesus think a four-day-old corpse could live again? How could Joshua have the audacity to ask the sun to stand still? They could ask the impossible of God because they were so oriented to God that they knew exactly what he was doing and what it meant. Elijah explained before the fire fell that God was turning Israel's heart back to him through the answer. Jesus declared, prior to raising Lazarus, that God was going to help those watching to believe. Joshua recognized that God was fighting for them through hailstones, then asked for more daylight to finish the job. In each instance these men were able to discern the activity, intent, or heart of God prior to asking. Because they knew what God wanted, he did what they asked.

Notice that their power with God flowed from a God-centered working relationship with God. What do I mean by a "working relationship"? Each of these saints paid the price in time, prayer, and sacrifice to under-stand God's perspective of their life and work. Once they understood it, they diligently set about their Father's business. As they poured out their lives in rolled-up sleeves, sweat, and service for his purposes, they felt God's power course through them. When this pattern of seeing as God sees and working with him became a day-in, day-out lifestyle, the Bible calls it "walking with God." In the book of Acts the entire church demonstrated this kind of relationship with God, and consequently the power of God flowed through the whole church.

The implication should be obvious. If you lead prayer, you must grasp this one truth above all others: *your primary job is to help the people of God be God-centered, to teach them that the primary purpose of prayer is a lifestyle of walking with God.* They must be oriented to him, not themselves. They must see life from his perspective rather than their own. They must understand his activity and what it means. Every time in Scripture and history that happened and the people responded, they saw the power of God. They saw it in individual lives, in small groups, in churches, in cities, and at times in an entire nation.

In all likelihood, if you don't have a dynamic prayer meeting this week, you won't have one next week. Teaching people how to orient their lives to God takes time. The upper room prayer meeting that preceded Pentecost was nestled in the context of three and one half years of the Son of God pouring his life into the disciples. That prayer meeting did not happen seven days after "Follow me." Jesus disciplined the hearts of the apostles until they walked with God. Then three thousand were converted in a day. Peter and John led the church to pray for boldness in the face of persecution, to resolve church conflict from God's perspective, and to experience other victories. Dynamic prayer meetings sprout from the soil of hearts that have been trained over time to become God-oriented.

One reason for the typical church prayer meeting anemia is how we've trained people to relate to God. The ones I've attended almost invariably consist of preaching/teaching followed by taking requests from the people and reviewing a prayer list. Perhaps the order's reversed, or a song or two may be added. This process varies in length but typically includes a pained look of pastoral concern from the leader as various members list those who are physically ill. Normally the somber tone concludes with a few key individuals or small groups reminding God of the requests just mentioned. The whole focus revolves around *our* wants, *our* needs, *our* concerns, and all of it from *our* perspective. After reviewing old concerns, we inject a few new ones, then proceed to ask God to do certain things according to our own understanding of how they ought to be done. In short, we have encouraged or allowed our people to be self-centered. Not surprisingly the working of God is barely seen in a desperate culture badly in need of his mighty power.

Foundation 2
Meaningful Relationships

In the early church, fervent prayer coursed through their spiritual veins in life-giving intimacy with the Father. Beyond intimacy lay power. Prayer did not result merely in their drawing closer to God but in God's power flowing through them. Quite a difference exists between sensing the love of God, learning new truths, and getting wisdom versus turning Jerusalem and Israel upside down.

Based on the pattern that power with God flows from a working relationship with God, I assumed that God poured out his might because the apostles prayed for and sought first the kingdom. When I began leading prayer meetings around the country, I advocated a format that called for praying for kingdom issues ahead of personal needs. In most churches, prayer meetings proved flat until participants began to pray for one another. This mystified me until I saw a dynamic in the book of Acts that explained the riddle. Indeed they did seek first the kingdom, but in order to seek first the kingdom a prior requirement had to be in place.

Let's take a look at three episodes from the life of the early church. In each event a common reality emerges related to what set the stage for power in prayer. What the believers did is set in small caps and what God did is in italics. See if you can diagnose the pattern.

Acts 2:42–47

And they [the new converts] continued
steadfastly in the apostles' doctrine and
FELLOWSHIP, in the BREAKING OF BREAD, and in
prayers. *Then* fear came upon every soul, and
many wonders and signs were done through the
apostles. Now all who believed were TOGETHER,
and HAD ALL THINGS IN COMMON, and sold
their possessions and goods, and DIVIDED THEM
AMONG ALL, as anyone had need.

So continuing daily with one accord in the
temple, and breaking bread FROM HOUSE TO
HOUSE, they ate their food with gladness and
simplicity of heart, praising God and having
favor with all the people. *And the Lord added* to
the church *daily* those who were being saved.

4:32–35

Now the multitude of those who believed
were of ONE HEART AND ONE SOUL; neither did
anyone say that any of the things he possessed
was his own, but THEY HAD ALL THINGS IN
COMMON. *And with great power* the apostles gave
witness to the resurrection of the Lord Jesus.
And great grace was upon them all. NOR WAS
THERE ANYONE AMONG THEM WHO LACKED; for
all who were possessors of lands or houses sold
them, and brought the proceeds of the things
that were sold, and laid them at the apostles'

feet; and they distributed to each AS ANYONE HAD NEED.

Acts 5:12–16, 41–42

And through the hands of the apostles *many signs and wonders were done* among the people. And they were all with ONE ACCORD IN SOLOMON'S PORCH. Yet none of the rest dared join them, but the people esteemed them highly. *And believers were increasingly added to the Lord,* multitudes of both men and women, so that THEY BROUGHT THE SICK OUT into the streets and laid them on beds and couches, that at least the shadow of Peter passing by might fall on some of them. Also a multitude gathered from the surrounding cities to Jerusalem, BRINGING SICK PEOPLE and THOSE WHO WERE TOR-MENTED BY UNCLEAN SPIRITS, *and they were all healed.* . . . So they departed from the presence of the council, rejoicing that they were counted worthy to suffer shame for His name. And DAILY in the temple, and IN EVERY HOUSE, they did not cease teaching and preaching Jesus as the Christ.

In each instance believers are loving one another. Notice that they shared possessions with one another, met daily in one another's homes and in the temple, were together in one accord, and brought out the sick and demon-oppressed. As a result, the Lord added daily those being saved, filled them with great power, great grace was upon them all, and they were all healed. God worked in their lives in proportion to the degree of the koinonia, the quality of love between believers. Their favor with God flowed largely from his pleasure of their depth of fellowship.

Dynamic prayer follows dynamic fellowship because we pray best with those we love most. Prayer rides the rails of relationship. Where relational conflict exists, believers cannot pray with one another. To a lesser degree, if you don't know someone well, you can't pray intimately with him. However, among those who have spent time together, eaten meals together, and sacrificed for one another, prayer is natural. We must indeed seek first the kingdom when we pray, but if we haven't paid the price to build deep relationships with those with whom we pray, then prayer will always lack depth. This truth was one of the key understandings that solved the mystery of why leading Christians from other churches to pray with one another for kingdom things rarely resulted in much passion. They didn't know one another. Over time I realized that rarely will persons seek first the kingdom with another Christian who does not share their hearts. Meaningful prayer follows meaningful relationships.

In church life the depth of corporate prayer will be in proportion to the depth of relationship believers have with one another. This means your prayer meetings will only be dynamic if you eat meals in one another's homes, enjoy fellowship time together, work on projects together, and give to one another. The only times I have ever seen a dynamism to prayer without first building relationships occurred around a critical issue on every-one's heart—the week after 9/11, for example. As a rule, however, you must build deep relationships among church members. You should ask questions like: "How much do people get together outside of church? How much time is spent in one another's homes? Do people bear one another's burdens?" Activities that encourage relationship-building set the stage for dynamic prayer meetings.

Foundation 3
The Leader's Walk with God

Can anyone give what he does not have, teach what he does not know, or lead where he has never been? The great leaders of Scripture and those today have learned how to walk with God. Guiding others in that same process merely flows from teaching them to do what the leader already does. Conversely, inability to function in God's presence will afflict those we lead with the same malady.

The ability to walk with God, to be God-centered, to discern his heart and interpret his activity comes only from God. Spirituality does not spring from any human wisdom or intelligence. Rather, God favors his servants and grants them the grace to know him. Solomon recognized this, and he pleaded at Gibeon, "Give to Your servant an understanding heart to judge Your people, that I may discern between good and evil. For who is able to judge this great people of Yours?" (1 Kings 3:9). Solomon did not turn to books to give him a five-step, how-to program; he turned to God. In the Hebrew the phrase "understanding heart" literally reads "a heart that hears." He knew that only God could give him the capacity to walk with him, be oriented to him, discern his wisdom, and know how to respond.

God doesn't distribute a discerning heart at random to everyone. At times he granted it to people; at times he withheld it. For example, Moses spoke to the children of Israel after leading them for forty years, "Yet the LORD has not given you a heart to perceive and eyes to see and ears to hear, to this very day" (Deut. 29:4). On the other hand, the Bible says of Lydia in Acts 16:14, "The Lord opened her heart to heed the things spoken by Paul." These dual examples are representative of the two-sided dealings of God. At times he grants these hearts; at times he leaves hearts hardened.

Obviously, there's a condition to be met, and God is not mysterious about what it is. He states it in many ways all across the pages of Scripture. One place where he sums it up succinctly is in Jeremiah 29:12–13: "Then you will call upon Me and go and pray to Me, and I will listen to you. And you will seek Me and find Me, when you search for Me with all your heart." *God limits a discerning heart to those who first have a seeking heart.* When the hearts of the people in Jesus' day grew dull, he told them parables precisely so they wouldn't be able to discern what his activity meant (Matt. 13:10–15). Conversely, the disciples were privileged to hear the secrets of the kingdom (Matt. 13:11, 16–17) because their hearts sought him. Do you see it? Seeking God with the whole heart results in God's granting the spiritual ability to walk with him. God doesn't cast pearls before swine; he doesn't let casual Christians who lack an intense hunger for him into his delights.

Why have I written about this at length? Because I don't want you to pick this book up as a how-to manual and bypass the relationship with God. This book can bear witness to some truths, but it cannot do what God reserves solely as his prerogative. If you want to see him, seek him. Seek him desperately in secret. Cry out to him; open your mouth and pant for him. Constantly monitor your heart's desire for him. Keep you finger on the pulse of desire to be with him. Make sure your hunger does not wane. Only by seeking God fervently, intensely, continually will you walk with God. Then and only then will those whom you lead walk with God. Then and only then will you discern the activity of God and see his power consistently.

If everything really does rise and fall on leadership, if we can't lead people where we ourselves have never been, or if those we lead become just like us, then let us lay aside the sin of sloth and distraction that so easily entangles us and run our race with perseverance. Let us not grow weary in matters of the heart. Let us guard our hearts with all diligence. May we stay before the flame of his Word until it ignites a fiery passion that cannot be quenched. May we reject the insistent voices that nibble away at the time spent with him, wall out the invading assaults of the lust of the flesh, the lust of the eyes, and the pride of life. May we deal harshly with the little indulgences that subvert our souls when their cumulative effect is to cool us spiritually! Only by so doing will we find the divine authority for leadership that flows from a life that loves God above all else.

One final comment: we must not wait on perfection before starting. Rather, the direction of our heart must be toward God resulting in increasing maturity.

Foundation 4
Hearts Right with God

God has always required a right heart, and all who miss it miss God. A Bible reader stumbles across it in the earliest scriptural foundations, as early as Cain and Abel. You see it in Genesis 4:3–5 as both brothers present the first recorded offerings to God. Immediately, the Bible tersely comments that God respected Abel and his offering, but God did not respect Cain and his offering. Notice that God's acceptance or rejection of the offering merely followed his acceptance or rejection of the person. God did not separate his willingness to respond from the condition of the heart of the one asking. This means God answers an individual or a church in proportion to how they are walking with him. He never differentiates between the thing requested and the one making the request. God doesn't answer prayer; he answers you. No amount of education, mastering a formula, or learning a certain skill set determines spiritual power in a prayer meeting; rather, God moves based on the hearts of the people praying.

A classic example of this occurred in a prayer meeting in the Hebrides Islands off the coast of Scotland. Christians there had been imploring God for some time to send revival and awakening. Finally, during a Friday night prayer meeting, a youth of sixteen prayed from Psalm 24, "Who may ascend into the hill of the LORD? Or who may stand in His holy place? He who has clean hands and a pure heart" (vv. 3–4). He then began to ask if his heart was pure. This led those praying to inspect their walk with God, to confess their sins, and to renew a right relationship with God. God began at that moment to transform those islands. In fact, as they were praying, God woke up most of the town at midnight, and they gathered at the village square asking how to be saved. Once the hearts of those Christians were cleansed, God worked mightily through them. Similarly, if you want to see the power of God in your prayer meetings, invest time in preparing the hearts of those whom you lead. The preparation will include a number of heart qualities that please God, such as thankfulness, holiness, responsiveness, humility, dependency, and worship. However,

I want to highlight two heart qualities required to start moving a powerless prayer meeting off dead center.

First, do you know the first words Jesus said to his disciples? Knowing where he began with them has great implications for where he begins with us. Scripture records that two of John's disciples followed Jesus based on his testimony. Jesus turns, sees them following him, and asks, "What do you seek?" (John 1:38). He could have introduced himself, written down their names, or made small talk before abruptly asking such a question. What was he doing? This prototype encounter tells us that the moment we approach Jesus, the first thing he gauges is our desire (seeking is a function of desire). We look for what we want. If we have no real desire, no hunger, we will never really pray with passion. James recognized this requirement and said, "The effective, *fervent* prayer of a righteous man avails much" (James 5:16). So integral is desire to prayer that one great prayer warrior of old defined *prayer* as "the soul's sincere desire." Not surprisingly, the prayer warriors of Scripture were passionate. They were intense. They were desperate. God had to come through, or they were finished. When we come to him in a prayer meeting, his scales weigh our desire, not our words. Prayer for the lost may be the will of God, but he won't respond to lips that pray dispassionately.

Second, 1 Corinthians 13 tells us that love is the greatest thing, but oddly enough Jesus never rebuked the disciples for their lack of it. However, four times in

Matthew alone he rebuked them for their lack of faith. When he began the transformation process with the disciples, he always pressed faith. He never pointed out great love in others, but he exalted the centurion and the woman with a demon-possessed son for their great faith.

Why did Jesus begin with faith if other virtues are greater? Precisely because faith, like desire, is a prerequisite. Neither rivals love for God, but you can't get there if you don't have them. They create the motion that readies us to walk with God. Great expectation moves us to lay hold of God until we encounter him, and without this faith it is impossible to please God. When you lead, you must fan the flames of faith until hearts truly believe that the omnipotent God of the universe is, and that he rewards those who diligently seek him.

A prayer request lacking intensity and expectation will get little response from God. These two attributes—faith and desire—set the stage to meet God, and in the average prayer meeting today they are desperately lacking.

One final note. Do not think that everyone in the church must be right with God. When a core group gets serious with God, he will move among his people.

Foundation 5
Believers in One Accord

Five times in the first five chapters of Acts, Scripture records that the disciples were in "one accord." In each instance the Greek word *homothumadon* is used. The word is a compound from *homos* meaning "same or together," and *thumos* meaning "passion, anger, fierceness, wrath, indignation, heat, or glow." Joining these concepts together, the word can be understood as the same burning of heart, or same heart passion. This ardor of heart unity, fellowship, and agreement in purpose, desire, passion, attitude, mentality, action, and lifestyle marked the dynamism of their prayer meetings (1:14 and 4:23 explicitly; 2:46 implicitly).

And the oxygen that fuels the flame of one accord above all else is purpose. Some years ago I read a book on prayer that said every prayer group must have a purpose for meeting or it will die. I can bear witness from personal experience the truth of that statement, but more importantly Scripture shows this to be true. Jesus never did anything without a purpose. His prayer life pulsated with passion for the reason of his earthly existence. In Acts 1 the apostles' prayer request to replace Judas flowed from their assignment as apostles. In Acts 4 they begged for boldness to proclaim Jesus. In Acts 13 one suspects "ministering to the Lord" means seeking clarity on what assignment he would give them next. This rich tapestry of prayer meetings was woven with the scarlet threads of heart purpose.

Being in one accord can take on at least two forms. First, it comes when a group has an incredible sense that they have been called by God. They clearly know their assignment, and they are seeking God's power and direction in carrying out his work. This form of one accord is a facet of Foundation 1, Relationship with God. Any group that passionately seeks to fulfill its assignment already has a sense of purpose and unity. The second type of accord can be more temporal in nature. In Acts 4:24 the entire church responded as one to the crisis. In your church or small group, you need both of these aspects of being in one accord. You must have a sense of purpose in general but also at the prayer meeting as people's hearts and understanding are touched in such a way that they come into agreement to pray. Unclear instruction or a halfhearted call to pray is ineffective in helping the hearts of people come together.

Evidently God especially loves to make us interdependent in fulfilling his purposes. Was that not the crux of the last verses in Jesus' high priestly prayer in John 17? Did he not pray for a oneness between himself and the Father, and among his followers? How else can you explain why he taught "If *two* of you agree . . ." (Matt 18:19)? When this happens, somehow it carries greater weight. T. W. Hunt wrote about how he unexpectedly discovered increased authority with the throne of God as the trial of cancer drove him and his wife into greater unity. Similarly, the greatest prayer times I've known have been when believers have come into a unity of heart passion, of being in one accord. This deepening in one accord over the long term follows a formula—an intensifying sense of purpose, plus trial, plus sacrificing for Christ's sake and for each other results in an increasingly deeper bond of love. The coming together in one accord at the moment of a prayer meeting follows this formula—a clear understanding of what is at stake, assuming personal responsibility, plus belief that God will answer when we cry. In the book of Acts, both these realities can be seen.

Foundation 6
Leader Responsibilities

Much of this book will address four leadership responsibilities, so I will expound on this principle in later chapters.

Conclusion

The purpose of this chapter is to identify the hidden foundations behind the façade of dynamic prayer meetings. Most of these dynamics have to do with Christians' relationship to God and with one another, not with a checklist for praying the "right" thing. Knowing how to relate to God and others is necessary for God to move.

CHAPTER 3

Your Four Responsibilities

Now for the million-dollar question: How do you get there? If we can't give up on our prayer meetings, then what can we do? No one simply wishes a dynamic prayer meeting into existence. Thankfully, the plan is not complicated. God did not create an enormously complex, mysterious system reserved for a select few. You don't need a PhD in quantum mechanics or to be a neurosurgeon. In fact, I'm convinced Scripture pictures only three desires of God and four responsibilities of a leader in prayer meeting.

The Three Desires of God

Carrier pigeons can be released miles away from their home. Without any map, flying over unfamiliar terrain through unforeseen challenges, they successfully follow an inner homing guide. Modern technology can do the same thing. Military missiles follow a guidance system to their targets. Once coordinates are locked in, the missile can start from any location and still be guided to its desired destination.

In a prayer meeting to know where to go, you must have a homing device—some overarching sense of how to lead people to a specific destination. Your guidance will come from knowing what God wants. You must always know how to answer the question, What motivates God to move dynamically in a prayer meeting? Why did he throw open prison doors (Acts 12:7) or shake the place where people were praying (Acts 4:31)? Why does he move in some circumstances and not in others? If you know what God wants, set your sails to the wind of his purpose. Scripture and history picture three basic desires of God that chart his course. One or all of these occur in dynamic prayer meetings.

1. *God wants to reveal himself to his people.* Why? When his people know him, they glorify him, learn to live in relationship with him, and become like him. Historically the great prayer meetings of awakenings resulted when God revealed himself to his people. In response they repented and were transformed into his image.

2. God wants to move his people onto his agenda. Why? When the people of God embrace his agenda, they get on mission with him; then he uses them to change the world. Acts 13:1–3 reflects how the Holy Spirit set apart Paul and Barnabas to the work to which he had called them and subsequently turned the world upside down.

3. God wants to build and minister to his people through his people. The result is koinonia, a deepening of the love believers have for one another. God can do anything in our lives independently of using another person; however, when he does it through another individual, our love for that person increases.

Your one purpose, your function as a leader, is merely to steer the ship in the direction of these three desires. The next logical question that follows is this: Practically, how do I walk with God in doing that?

The Four Responsibilities

You have four responsibilities in order to fulfill God's purposes. In order of importance, they are:

- *Discerning* the activity of God
- *Shepherding* the people of God
- Designing a God-centered *format*
- Facilitating *activities* that involve participants

As we consider these responsibilities, we will validate their biblical basis, briefly explain each one, lightly comment on how their interdependencies work, and introduce a worksheet that will help you design your own prayer meeting. In short, this one chapter will preview the lion's share of what follows in this book.

The clearest biblical picture of these four responsibilities occurs in Solomon's temple dedication ceremony. I am exalting him as the paradigm that best conveys how a leader functions. This ceremony paints a picture of the dynamics of the four responsibilities. In this picture you can see:

1. Solomon kneeling on the bronze platform he built with his hands raised to heaven.
2. Behind him in an arc, the children of Israel bowing with their faces to the ground.
3. In front of Solomon will be the bronze altar with fire falling out of heaven, burning up the sacrifices.
4. Behind the altar will be the temple filled with smoke.
5. Somewhere in the picture needs to be the 120 priests holding their trumpets and the musicians playing their instruments.
6. Write in four quadrants these phrases respectively: Discerning the Activity of God, Shepherding the People of God, a God-Centered Format, Activities That Involve.

Now let's unpack each one.

Responsibility 1: Discerning the Activity of God

Team sports require great coordination among players. In football the quarterback actually throws the ball before the receiver makes his cut. That means the receiver must understand the play called by the quarterback. Failure to do so results in an incompletion or, worst yet, an interception.

A servant must know what his master is doing. Leading a prayer meeting requires that you know the general direction God already wants to go or that you know how to recognize when he starts to reveal it. Otherwise you will be leading in the wrong direction. The result will be failure to connect. For example, suppose God wants the church to reach out to inner-city children, but the church wants to start a resort ministry. Could they plan a prayer meeting asking amiss and expect God to move? What if God wanted to change the format of the prayer meeting by reaching out to one of his own who is hurting? Would God likely respond if we missed what was on his heart because we were trying to get through an agenda? Therefore, it is critical to discern God's activity.

Watch how Solomon planned and led the prayer meeting based on discerning God's activity. First, he planned based on what God had already been doing. He recounted God's leading through his father David, the ordaining of building the temple, and his being chosen to do it (2 Chron. 6:4–11). He designed the service to fall in line with what God had already been doing. Second, as the service progressed, two things happened that he could not have programmed. The presence of God filled the temple (2 Chron. 5:13), and God dropped fire out of heaven to burn up the sacrifices (2 Chron 7:1). Wouldn't it have been foolish for Solomon to have ignored that? He immediately changed his format and guided (shepherded) the people in their understanding and response. He answered by declaring, "The LORD said He would dwell in the dark cloud" (2 Chron. 6:1). Then he allowed space for the people to respond by bowing, worshipping, and praising God (2 Chron. 7:3).

In prayer meeting you will plan the format based on discerning God's activity. You will meditate on his purposes and make the connection to how he's been carrying that out among those whom you shepherd. Once the prayer meeting begins, you must also be ready to adjust your plans if God works in an unexpected way. God doesn't always change the meeting, but if he does, you must respond.

Responsibility 2: Shepherding the Heart of the People of God

If God made you a spiritual leader, what does he want you to do? Let's look at a defining moment in the life of Peter (John 21). Jesus creates an encounter with Peter to drive home a point. Watch how he does it. Peter returns to fishing—not what Jesus has in mind for his life. He's caught nothing all night, but then a stranger appears and advises the men to cast their net on the right side of the boat. The huge catch duplicated Peter's original call in Luke 5, no doubt calling it to mind. On shore Jesus has fish laid on a "fire of coals." The only other time this phrase occurs in the Bible is when Peter warmed his hands over a "fire of coals" at Annas's house. Then Jesus asked three times if he loved him, just as Peter had denied three times that he knew him. No doubt the fire of coals and the three questions must have taken him back to his denial. Jesus does it not to condemn him but to reaffirm his purpose for Peter's life. He's dealing with the guilt in the context of Peter's original call. He's about to reinstate him, particularly as a leader. This scenario Jesus deliberately brought about has a repeated refrain. Three times Jesus called his people sheep, and three times he called Peter to function as a shepherd as the way he wished to be loved. *If Peter really loved him, he should shepherd his sheep.*

If you lead the people of God, Jesus especially wants you to love him by shepherding his sheep. We see from Peter's example that shepherding is the primary function of a leader with the people of God. So intrinsic is shepherding to leadership that throughout the Bible God calls his leaders shepherds. Jesus, the great Shepherd, has charged pastors (the word literally means "shepherds") to work with him as "undershepherds," to help the people of God walk with him. In a prayer meeting we "undershepherd" by guiding people into the three desires of God. You point out how God is revealing himself, guide people onto God's agenda, and create opportunities for them to minister to one another.

Notice how Solomon did it. He spoke words and acted in ways that oriented the people to God. When the cloud filled the temple during prayer meeting, Solomon responded by quoting to the people what God had said about dwelling in a dark cloud (2 Chron. 6:1–2); then he blessed the people (v. 3), and then he recounted the activity of God (vv. 4–11). Additionally, his lengthy prayer in 6:14–42 would have helped people better understand the ways of God and how to relate to him. All of these actions shepherded their hearts toward God. The people understood God's revelation of himself and affirmed God's agenda of the temple.

Responsibility 3: Designing a God-Centered Format

A format is the template for how you plan the prayer meeting. It organizes your themes and time. The themes you choose will tremendously help or hinder your people being God-centered. If you spend most of your time reviewing a prayer list or taking needs from the group, most likely the people will be needs-focused. If you spend most of the time bearing witness to God's activity, his mission, his purposes, his character, his promises, and his answers, then most likely your people will be God-centered.

The format you use will be one of the greatest human tools at your disposal for shepherding. A good format will set the stage for encountering God, fulfilling the three great desires of God, and recognizing his activity among the people.

Look at the format Solomon chose for the temple dedication.

1. He set the focus on God through singing and a procession of the priests (2 Chron. 5:1–13).
2. He responded to the cloud by declaring what it meant, blessed the people, and declared the activity of God that brought them to this point (2 Chron. 5:13–6:11).
3. He offered a prayer of invocation/dedication (2 Chron. 6:12–42).
4. He led people to respond to God (2 Chron. 7:1–4).
5. He blessed the people and offered sacrifices (1 Kings 8:55–64).

The first part of the format had different segments of time given to specific activities such as singing, blowing trumpets, and a processional march. The cumulative effect would have been to fix people's attention on God, prepare their hearts for meeting God, and orient them to God's purposes—to help them become God-centered. The second part of the format guided them in understanding God's revelation of himself in the cloud.

In the third part he beseeched the Lord to sanctify his temple as a house of prayer according to God's purposes. In the fourth part he either led or allowed room for the people to respond to the fire of God falling from heaven. Finally, the last record of the day was that he blessed the people and offered sacrifices.

Solomon's format was designed to orient people to God. His focus activities and prayer times led them to concentrate on the Father. You must design a format that does the same.

What format does the Bible prescribe? After studying all the prayer meetings in Scripture, I do not find that it advocates one. God does not say, "Thus saith the Lord, thou shalt have this format." Instead variety exists. That means the unchanging principles can be expressed in changeable formats. That being acknowledged, I'm proposing one as a model for the remainder of this book. I do not believe it to be the only option, but learning cannot occur without a reference point. By considering a concrete example, you can better grasp the principles behind it. If God does lead you to adjust the format in your situation, you will have a better idea of how to do that.

The one-hour model format consists of five segments: Focus on God, Respond from the Heart, Seek First the Kingdom, Present Your Requests, and Close in Celebration.

A One-Hour Format

- Focus on God
- Respond from the heart
- Seek first the kingdom
- Present your requests
- Close in celebration

Focus on God: 10–15 minutes

I will briefly explain each segment and its primary purpose.

In the opening bell of a prayer meeting, the leader must start with God if the rest of the hour is to be God-centered. Begin with a time of music, Scripture, or testimony so that people focus on God. Pray ahead of time and ask God what aspect(s) about himself he wants you to highlight. Typically, you will sense one primary thought, such as who God is, what he can do, the nature of his love, or his mission. You will exalt this truth about him or his activity in this segment. You should allow ten to fifteen minutes to do this.

Primary purpose: To help hearts get oriented to and prepared for meeting God.

Respond from the Heart: 10 minutes

Whenever the people of God truly focus on God, their hearts respond. In the Bible the response varied; sometimes it was thanksgiving, sometimes conviction of sin, sometimes increased faith, or a host of other reactions. But since God is after the heart, he impacts the heart. You need to give your people time to respond to him. They can do this in any number of ways, including silent prayer, group prayer, and singing, but you are creating the time for the Holy Spirit's work in the hearts of his people.

Primary purpose: To let the heart of God's people respond to him.

Seek First the Kingdom: 20–25 minutes

In the Lord's Prayer Jesus taught us to pray for the kingdom before we asked for our daily bread. He encouraged beginning with the agenda of God instead of our agenda. This makes logical sense for a relationship marked by love. Love puts the other first, so this is our natural response to all that God has done for us. We put his agenda/desires/purposes ahead of our own. Jesus concluded the chapter by telling us if we sought the kingdom first, God would meet our needs. By creating this as a segment, you build a platform into the prayer meeting to move people to God's agenda. You will pray for the things of God such as the lost, missions, koinonia among believers, the upcoming VBS, and ministry to the homeless. You will exalt the things that edify the church and reach the world.

Primary purpose: To help the people of God be on God's agenda.

Present Your Requests: 10–15 minutes

Here you create a segment to pray for the needs and concerns of the people. You will lift up the sick, the hurting, and personal requests. You do this through activities which involve all the people in ministering to one another. In chapter 5 you will find practical suggestions to handle prayer requests so the focus on God is not lost.

Primary purpose: To let people minister to one another by praying for one another.

Close in Celebration: 5 minutes

After spending time in the presence of God, encountering his goodness, casting our burdens on him, being built up, and having our relationship renewed afresh from his touch, then the people of God usually will want to respond with thanksgiving or celebration. Some type of closing in which their hearts can praise or thank God is appropriate. Often music will be a good way to do this.

Primary purpose: To let people affirm the blessing of having been in God's presence.

Responsbility 4: Facilitating Activities That Involve Participants

In the end you must have practical ways that guide people to respond to God, get on his agenda, and minister to one another. The activities you choose can greatly aid or hinder that process. The specific activities you can do are endless, but after listening to many prayer leaders across the country, I believe three main types exist—focusing, participating, and ministering.

Focusing Activities

Any activity that focuses the people on God falls into this category. The possibilities are extensive, a few examples being the leader's words, reading Scripture, singing, testimony, drama, and carrying banners. Especially use these types of activities at the beginning of prayer meeting when you are seeking to set the focus on God. Continue orienting people to God as you progress through the prayer meeting. Under the guidance of the Holy Spirit, select what's appropriate for your prayer meeting.

Primary purpose: To orient participants to God by setting or maintaining the focus on God.

Participating Activities

Any activity that requires participation from the people falls in this category. According to Ephesians 4:11–12, God did not call the leader to do the work of ministry. He called the leader to equip the people of God to do the work of ministry. This means you cannot be the show. You must create activities that allow all the people to play a part. Usually you see his activity most when each member participates. The best way to create participation is to involve as many people as you can both numerically and physically.

Numerically. Every person in the prayer meeting needs to do something. You can give away leadership roles in various ways such as having a number of participants read Scripture, give testimonies, and guide prayer times. You can involve everyone else through activities such as singing, small groups, individually praying out loud all at once, responsive reading, or large-group sentence prayer. But everybody needs to do something. No one should be denied the chance to participate.

Physically. People's bodily participation often encourages their hearts to participate. Use various activities that require physical movement such as coming to the altar, kneeling, writing a prayer card, holding hands, standing to pray with another, or breaking into small groups. Too many prayer meetings encourage spectator mode by allowing people to sit there. If you engage their bodies, their hearts are more likely to engage.

Primary purpose: To involve as many people as possible, both numerically and physically.

Ministering Activities

Any activity that causes people to minister to one another falls into this category. The equipping of the saints in Ephesians 4:12 is for the edifying of the body. Therefore, you need to encourage activities that allow the people to do just that. You could do things such as kneeling beside one another at the altar, having new mothers stand and the congregation pray for them, having participants put their hands on one another's shoulders, having the church surround someone with a special need, having small groups lay hands on those with cancer, having members pray in pairs for each other. Incorporate these activities into the format to let the body build itself up in love.

Primary purpose: For the body to minister to and build itself up in love.

Notice that the Bible pictures Solomon shepherding the people through activities. The trumpet playing, the explanation of God's working, and the prayers were focusing activities. Next he involved the priests, musicians, trumpeters, Levites, and the people in numerical and physical participation activities. He gave away multiple leadership roles and led all the people to respond. He facilitated their bodily involvement through standing, bowing, speaking, and singing. Finally, you can see a ministering activity as he blessed the people.

Designing a Prayer Meeting

I've broken down the four responsibilities of the leader into respective categories. However, leading the actual prayer meeting is not a mechanical, sequential-step, awkward, rigid, stand-alone process. It's much like swimming. The arms, legs, breathing, and timing produce the fluid motion of swimming when all of them work seamlessly. So it is with leading prayer meeting. What you do requires the interdependencies of all four responsibilities.

The template on pages 68 and 69 is designed to help you take these four responsibilities and put them together fluidly and practically. You will design your prayer meeting by taking themes and activities from 68 and filling them in on page 69. You may notice that Discerning and Shepherding do not appear in the template. This is because they are the guides for the themes of the Format and the Activities you choose.

I once led a prayer conference in North Carolina in which God moved powerfully. It followed this template, and here is how it worked.

1. We focused on God. We began by singing. This was followed by a brief exhortation from Hebrews 6:13–18 to prepare hearts to believe God.

2. We responded from the heart. We read Psalm 103 and spent time responding to God by blessing him. We did this in sentence prayers saying, "Father, I bless you for . . ." and named the things he had done for us.

3. We sought first the kingdom. Those with burdens who desired a special touch from God were invited to come to the front. Others who felt led knelt beside them and prayed for them. People began to ask if they could testify of what God had done or said to them recently (I had not planned for this, but it happened). Then we prayed for kingdom concerns in small groups. Some people asked for a special prayer for their churches (also not planned on my part).

4. We presented our requests. We prayed for a series of personal concerns in small groups or pairs.

5. We closed in celebration. We sang "To God Be the Glory."

Discerning the activity of God came in when people began testifying and asking special prayer. In this instance God was touching hearts, and people were responding to him. I changed what I had planned to do next on the format. Shepherding occurred by encouraging faith from Hebrews 6:13–18, praising God from Psalm 103, and

Two Pillars of a Prayer Meeting

GOD-CENTERED FORMAT	INVOLVEMENT ACTIVITIES

Focus on God
- Who he is
- What he can do
- His presence
- Getting his perspective
- Hearing his voice

Respond from the heart
- Becoming God-centered
- Exercising faith
- Honesty with God
- Repentance
- Dependence on God
- Praise

Seek first the kingdom
- Pray for one another's spiritual walk
- Pray for the backslidden
- Pray for the lost
- Pray for missions
- Pray for awakening
- Pray for VBS

Present your requests
- Sick
- Financial
- Jobs
- Other personal concerns

Close in celebration
- Thanksgiving
- Proclamation
- Praise
- Declaration

Focusing
- Leader's words
- Scripture
- Music
- Testimony
- Drama

Participation activities
NUMERICALLY
- Ask people to have different roles in leading, testifying, reading Scripture, etc.
- Singing
- Small groups
- Praying aloud all at once
- Responsive reading
- Large group sentence prayer, etc.

PHYSICALLY
- Come to the altar
- Kneel
- Stand in pairs
- Banner rotation
- Go to someone else during the prayer meeting
- Writing a prayer card note
- Prayerwalking

Ministering Activities
- Prayer chair
- Pray for focus group like new mothers or mission team
- Have people pray for and bless one another by name
- Coming to the altar

Your Plan for a Prayer Meeting

GOD-CENTERED FORMAT	INVOLVEMENT ACTIVITIES

Focus on God

1. _____   _____

Respond from the heart

1. _____   _____

Seek first the kingdom

1. _____   _____

2. _____   _____

3. _____   _____

4. _____   _____

Present your requests

1. _____   _____

2. _____   _____

Close in celebration

1. _____   _____

guiding people to minister to one another at the front and in small groups. The format started with God, guided people to respond to him, and involved kingdom concerns. Finally, the activities of singing, reading Scripture, testifying, coming to the altar, and breaking into small groups involved all participants.

Conclusion

You have just seen in one chapter an overview of the heart of the book. Over the next four chapters we will sequentially examine in detail each of the four responsibilities and how to execute them.

CHAPTER 4

Designing a God-Centered Format

Now it's time for nuts and bolts. The first three chapters laid foundations and gave you the big-picture overview. In the next four we will focus on practices, examples, and leadership tips.

Lurking in every format is the insidious promise of God-in-a-box programming, but as you can tell from the chapter title, that's where we're beginning. Smacks of hypocrisy, does it not—to say one thing and do another? Worse yet, in the last chapter I insinuated that the format merely girds the towel of service to wash the feet of discerning the activity of God and shepherding the people of God. I suppose an explanation is in order. Why in the world would I reverse the order and begin with something of lesser importance, something that will not work unless the responsibilities of discerning and shepherding are in place?

Because of experience gained from teaching leaders how to lead prayer meetings. Have you ever been wrong because you were right? Oddly enough, I made a mistake early on based on a correct assumption. I rightly knew that God responds to the heart, not the details of executing a certain prescribed format. For example, the prayer meetings in Ezra 8:21–24, Nehemiah 9:5–38, and Acts 13:1–3 vary from one another. Fasting proved integral to Ezra, confession of sin to Nehemiah, and seeking the mind of God for Paul. This diversity proves that God doesn't interact with his people based on one single pattern but on his purpose and the response of the people. Just as we don't conduct human relationships by rigid, inflexible formulas, neither will our relationship with God at a prayer meeting be rigid or inflexible. Sometimes God may change or interrupt the format, and the most important requirement of leadership is to know how to adjust to him.

Knowing this, I deliberately (albeit mistakenly) chose not to give a format; instead I talked solely about the heart principles that please God. After four weeks everyone in the class had that classic deer-in-the-headlights expression. When one student has that look, it's probably the fault of the student. When the whole class has that look, it's the fault of the teacher. That experience taught me an invaluable lesson: even though dynamic prayer is predicated on the heart, you must begin teaching a format to create a reference point for learning. Once people grasp a certain pattern, it generates talking points so they can more readily grasp how to discern and shepherd. It's much akin to a driver's education class. Could you imagine the teacher lecturing without mentioning the ignition, the gear shift, the steering wheel, the gas pedal, and the brake? Ultimately, you want the student to drive, not focus on car parts. But without a working knowledge of the automobile, they would have no basis to comprehend what you were talking about. So we begin with format for order of learning, not order of importance.

That cornerstone of understanding being laid, let's turn our attention to the format introduced in the last chapter. Our one-hour model is divided into five segments that loosely follow the Lord's Prayer. They are:

- Focus on God
- Respond from the heart
- Seek first the kingdom
- Present your requests
- Close in celebration

Let's examine each of these in detail.

Focus on God (10–15 minutes)

The purpose of this segment is to work with God in orienting people to him, to help prepare their hearts to pray from a God-centered viewpoint.

In construction the foundation determines whether the rest of the building will be right. Similarly the foundation you lay in the first ten to fifteen minutes of the prayer meeting will tremendously impact whether you encounter God. As a leader you must know where and how to start. A great example of what to do occurs in Acts 4:23–24. Peter and John have just been threatened with death because of the miracle performed on the lame man. They report it to the church and then lead a prayer meeting. Logically speaking, how would you expect them to begin such a critical prayer time? The obvious need is for protection and deliverance, but they do not start there. Instead, verse 24 records that the first words out of their mouths were, "Lord, You are God, who made heaven and earth and the sea, and all that is in them." Strange isn't it—to have a death threat looming over their heads and to start with God as Creator? Why would they do that?

Peter and John faced the temptation to focus on their struggle for life; instead they choose to focus on the Creator who determined their life. The three years with Jesus had thoroughly trained them to center on God more than the storm, the crowds, the detracting Pharisees, the lack of bread, or anything else. When the Sanhedrin threatened them, they instinctively practiced this truth. In effect they said, "Let's see—on the one hand we have someone who can take our lives, telling us to shut up; on the other hand we have the One who gives life, telling us to shout out!" By focusing on God, they were able to gain the perspective of God regarding their situation. It so informed their understanding that they requested boldness, not protection.

The first thing you must do as a leader is to set the focus on God. This opening segment is the most critical part of the prayer meeting. If the people don't move from a self-orientation to a God-orientation in the first few minutes, they likely will not encounter God the rest of the prayer meeting. Not surprisingly, throughout the Bible leaders spent a considerable amount of time making sure the people were ready to meet God. Pouring fresh water into a dirty cup neither cleans the cup nor makes the water potable.

So it is with prayer. If the people are filled with fears, needs, misconceptions, agendas, selfish desires, personal ambition, or any other focus, they are no more fit to connect with God's presence than the cup to receive clean water. Most people come to prayer meetings with their minds somewhere else. They may still be dwelling on the last thing at work, reeling from the scurry of trying to get the kids fed and loaded into the car to make it on time, or daydreaming about what will happen on the weekend. Because of this, I do not recommend immediately beginning a prayer meeting in prayer. First, hearts and minds must be set on God in order to pray.

Setting the focus on God should require about ten to fifteen minutes. Practically speaking, how do you do that? Three rules will help guide you.

Rule 1: Ask God

Pray to plan your prayer meeting. Often God will bring to your mind at least one truth about him to highlight, such as his nature, desires, likes, dislikes, perspective, activity, standards, purposes, attributes, intentions, or promises. You don't have to create a sermon or teach a lesson, but you will identify how you will briefly talk about this from God's perspective. In Acts 4:24–28 you can see how God impacted Peter and John's minds regarding his sovereignty. They reiterated his omnipotence, demonstrated in creation, that he predicted through David there would be conflict and that he let the Hebrew leaders succeed as far as they did only because it fulfilled his plan. All of this gave them the proper perspective regarding God's being in control of their situation and the resolve to do his will despite persecution. Your prayer meetings may not have as much riding on the line, but the principle is the same: God will impact minds and hearts through what you share to prepare the people to pray.

I mentioned in chapter 1 a prayer meeting in Woodstock, Georgia, that radically impacted the participants. Let me tell you more about that meeting. I met with Bruce Schmidt, the minister of prayer at First Baptist Woodstock, that morning to pray. When

I arrived, he was weeping. He said, "You probably don't know me well enough to know that I almost never weep, but God really impressed on me that Mother's Day is not a joyous occasion for many women. I just received a letter from a woman who gave up her son for adoption when she was a teenager, lamenting how that day reminded her of a son with whom she had no relationship. Then I thought about other women who have had abortions or children who have died, and I realized that it's a difficult time for many women."

By touching Bruce's heart, God was alerting him that he wanted Bruce to minister to his people. Bruce prayed that God would reveal someone who could give an appropriate testimony that evening and lead a prayer time. By the end of the day, God had provided three different women to give testimonies addressing those situations! That evening they gave a testimony, and God powerfully ministered to women who had experienced those situations.

Note: the one exception I've seen about preplanning a prayer meeting occurs when a group of Christians are so mature they know how to enter God's presence together and hear him dictate the agenda. Lucius, Simeon, Niger, Barnabas, and Saul are biblical examples of this in Acts 13. Most Christians, though, don't know how to function that way and will need proactive leadership.

Rule 2: Choose the means

How do people focus on God? God may guide using any number of means, but typically three will be staples—Scripture, testimony, and music.

Scripture

Notice that the apostles quoted Psalm 2:1, "Who by the mouth of Your servant David have said: 'Why did the nations rage, and the people plot vain things?'" (Acts 4:25). Quoting or being guided by Scripture is common in the prayers of the Bible. This pattern should inform any leader that God uses Scripture to shape the prayer meeting, and it demonstrates how he uses it. When you read Scripture, you want to do one or more of the following:

1. *Speak from God's perspective regarding how he acts, thinks, responds, prefers, wants, likes, dislikes, or what his purposes are.* The quote from Psalm 2:1 showed God's purposes and perspective regarding the early church's circumstances. Sometimes you will have a specific word as the apostles did; other times you may give a general truth about God. For example, if you felt God leading you to encourage faith in him, you could read Hebrew 11:6 and contrast it with Matthew 21:22. Then you might say something like, "According to Hebrews 11:6, what is the likelihood that God will be pleased if we don't have faith? According to Matthew 21:22, what is the likelihood that he will be pleased if we do? Since God wrote these verses and many others, what would his

motive be that we 'get it' when it comes to faith? He must have overly emphasized the requirement of faith to ensure that we wouldn't misunderstand how important it is to him and how intensely he desires his people to experience him and his blessings. On a scale of 1 to 10, what is the likelihood that he will do exactly that right now?"

2. *Show how God's current activity corresponds to his pattern of activity in Scripture.* Of course, that happened at the prayer meeting in Acts 4, but an expanded example occurred on the day of Pentecost. In Acts 2 Peter quoted from several passages to help them make the connection between what God said or did in Scripture to what was happening in their day. If God has done something in the life of the church, help the people see how his current activity is like what he did in Scripture.

You may also tell what God's future actions will be like based on what he has done in the past. I remember the cry of a lady in her sixties at a prayer conference. The message of 2 Chronicles 7:13–14 had just concluded, clearly showing that our nation is under God's judgment but also that God is extending to us his invitation to repent so that he might heal our land. The presence of the Lord fell mightily, and many tears began to flow as people were seized with conviction.

This dear lady especially was gripped with the sense of impending judgment, and she began to plead with God for mercy. All she could do for some time was repeat between sobs, "O God, my grandchildren! O God my grandchildren!" She saw the pattern of how

God judged sin in Scripture and what that means in our day. She also knew that just as God had been merciful so many times in the past, he might hear her cry for the land where her grandchildren would grow up.

3. *Clearly communicate the relevance and how God wants everyone to respond.* In the prayer meeting in Acts 4, Peter and John gave the "so what" in verses 29–30: "Now, Lord, look on their threats, and grant to Your servants that with all boldness they may speak Your word, by stretching out Your hand to heal, and that signs and wonders may be done through the name of Your holy Servant Jesus." In light of Scripture the church knew clearly what they ought to pray for and how they should react.

4. *When you don't have a specific word from God, use Scripture to highlight a truth about God or to stir expectation about what God could do.* For example, you could read John 14:13, "And whatever you ask in My name, that I will do, that the Father may be glorified in the Son." You might then just raise questions: "What does 'whatever' mean? Could God have a plan for our church, or are we too small? Could he do it through a handful who really believe him, or does he need more people? Could he do something in the next week? Well, he could. At this moment we may not know what he will do, or when he will do it, or how he will do it, but we know all things are possible with him. Are you ready to meet him tonight? We're not advocating name-it-and-claim-it, but we expect that he's going to use us to make a difference."

Testimony

In Acts 4:27–28 Peter and John declared, "For truly against Your holy Servant Jesus, whom You anointed, both Herod and Pontius Pilate, with the Gentiles and the people of Israel, were gathered together to do whatever Your hand and Your purpose determined before to be done." We now read this statement in the Bible, but it was not Bible for the people who lived it. Nowhere in the Old Testament did God record by name that Pilate and Herod would crucify Jesus. No, this was testimony for them. They bore witness to the current activity of God in their day. Few things make Scripture come alive more than a real-life example of God's working. In this prayer meeting they combined Scripture and testimony as a way to help the church be oriented to God.

When giving a testimony, remember a couple of guidelines.

1. *Make sure that God is the central player in the story.* Some people give testimonies in such a way that the focus falls on them. It's OK to talk about oneself if it magnifies the contrast between God and oneself or makes his activity clearer. For example: "I sensed God wanted me to witness to this man. I'm not good with words, and I stumbled the whole way through; but at the end of it, tears began streaming down his face, as he confessed his sin and turned to God. I was dumbfounded. I knew I didn't do that. Only God could do that. He really didn't need my eloquence, only my willingness."

In this example the person mentions himself but in a way that magnifies the activity of God.

2. *Make sure the testimony's relevance is clear.* When someone gives a testimony, it ought to direct the hearts of the hearers for what will be prayed about. I remember one particularly powerful prayer meeting I attended. The doctors had diagnosed a young lady with terminal cancer. Perhaps two hundred people gathered for a special service to ask God to heal her. During the prayer service another lady who had cancer shared how the doctors also gave her just months to live. That was seven years ago, and she was still going strong. The cancer remained present in her body, but a chemo regimen had kept it in check. Her testimony relevantly, powerfully encouraged us to look to God as we began to pray.

3. *When someone gives a testimony, make sure you stand ready to keep the focus on God.* Some people don't know how to get started, and they certainly don't know how to quit. They may chase rabbits or drag on mercilessly. You can avoid this situation by recruiting someone ahead of time and coaching them on how to glorify God. If you have an open time of sharing, be ready to gently redirect the focus on God by asking questions of the person giving the testimony. When he or she chases a rabbit, you may ask a question like, "And how did God's working impact you? What does he want us to learn? Can you tell us what the bottom line is that we need to know right now to pray?"

Music

Music can be a marvelous aid in turning the heart toward God. The ways music may be used are endless. Many leaders choose a couple of opening songs during this segment, and often they continue to use music throughout the prayer meeting. You may preplan some songs, pick a theme that you sing as a refrain throughout the prayer meeting, or play instrumental music while members pray. If you are in a small group, members may just sing what comes to mind, and others in the group may join in. When you use music, keep these suggestions in mind.

1. *Make sure the music is not just rote.* Don't let people sing without their minds being engaged.

2. *Pick music that fits with what you sense God is saying.* For small groups this won't require much structure, but if you lead a larger audience, this may take some coordination with a music leader, depending on your preference.

3. *Let music prepare hearts or be an expression as a response of the heart.* Singing in this opening segment prepares hearts by orienting people to God. Singing during or at the end of the prayer meeting leads the heart to respond to God.

I saw a wonderful example of preparing hearts with music and testimony at my church. The worship leader had us sing "Great Is Thy Faithfulness." After the first stanza he interrupted the song. From the audience a young mother, Delinia, walked to the platform and began to relate a recent crisis concerning her baby, her firstborn. A few weeks earlier the little girl, Paige, had run a high fever for seven days. Finally she and her husband took her to the hospital for tests. While there the baby worsened, lying limply against her mother as the hospital workers desperately searched for the cause of the deadly disease. She began tenderly stroking her daughter's head in an effort to console her. Suddenly, she noticed a protrusion at the soft spot—an indication of swelling of the brain.

The doctor suspected bacterial meningitis, a lethal killer or crippler. The tests proved positive, and immediately they began to administer intravenous antibiotics. Needle sticks on infants sometimes prove troublesome, easily working themselves out of small veins, and unfortunately Paige experienced this complication. About that time some of Delinia's friends heard the news and rushed to the hospital to pray for her. They asked God to let the next needle stay put and that the baby would suffer no ill effects from the meningitis. Almost always needles do not stay past ten days in babies, but the next one lasted fourteen days until the nurse had to pull it out at the time of Paige's discharge! Regarding any permanent damage, the doctors concluded that the weeklong illness must have lowered Paige's immune system, making her susceptible, but she probably didn't contract meningitis until just before she went to the hospital. That means they caught the disease in its initial stage, and her baby suffered no ill effects whatsoever! She finished the testimony and returned to her seat as the music leader led the congregation to sing the last stanza and chorus of "Great Is Thy Faithfulness": "Morning by morning new mercies I see: All I have needed, Thy hand has provided; Great is Thy faithfulness, Lord unto me."

When we finished singing, everyone was focused on God! We were ready to meet him.

Other Means

You can also use drama, banners, video clips, radio sound bites, or any number of things. Whatever focuses people on God is fine to do.

Rule 3: Avoid things that undercut focus

1. *Lack of energy.* As a leader you set the tone by how you start. You influence others' expectation by your expectation. If you really believe you have entered into the presence of the Almighty, the living God, who loves you completely, who has the power to do anything, who has promised that power to those who seek first his kingdom, then your demeanor ought to communicate that. All things are possible with God, but have you ever heard prayer meetings begun like this: "We are few tonight, but I appreciate your being here. You're the faithful ones who made it through the rain. Well, what do we want to pray for tonight? Do we have anyone in the hospital?" That doesn't help. Prayer meetings ought to carry the expectation of a delivery room instead of a hospital morgue.

2. *Taking prayer requests from a large group.* This typically kills the focus on God. Participants don't usually give the requests with a God focus; instead they most often focus on the need. Furthermore, to listen to how people give a prayer request, one would think a direct inverse proportion exists between how bad it sounds and the likelihood of God's answering. The nature of the beast demands the horrid particulars be rehearsed in excruciating detail. Also in every prayer meeting, at least one rabbit chaser raises a hand and then, having gained the floor, gives the request along with the history of the whole family tree. For some it's just exciting to hear oneself talk, and they enjoy the attention harvested from the field of a captive audience.

If you have just set the focus on God and then turned it over to this environment, it will scuttle a God-centeredness. Not only do you get a subversive effect from these requests individually, but taken as a whole, they have a life of their own. When you string together one after another, the cumulative effect sets a man/needs-centered tone, not to mention the time it robs from prayer.

3. *Most prayer lists.* Prayer lists and prayer requests from a large group are first cousins. If you set the focus on God and then you focus on a list, ticking off one request after another, you will most likely contract PMDS—prayer meeting depression syndrome. Have you ever been to a prayer meeting where you felt worse after attending than before you went? My father jokingly

used to say, "If you're ever feeling good and want to get over it, go to the Wednesday night prayer meeting. It's the most depressing time in all of church life." That's because the God-centeredness languishes.

Prayer lists often morph into a life of their own. One pastor told me that they decided to clean up their prayer list one night at prayer meeting. The backlog included requests such as "please pray for tomorrow's emergency open-heart surgery" listed four months earlier, and a ten-month old plea for a safe pregnancy of somebody's friend's sister's cousin. However, the winner was someone who had been on their list for eighteen months, but nobody knew who they were or who had even put them there.

What do you do about the prayer list? If next week you were to say to your congregation, "I've just discovered that our prayer list is killing the focus on God. We're going to get rid of it," what would happen to you? You would either need to start looking for another church, or you would experience a massive drop in attendance. Why? Because to the people with their name on that list, you are communicating that you love them. There are certain ways to deal with both prayer lists and prayer requests so that people are ministered to, but the focus on God is not hijacked.

Chapter 8, "Making the Transition," will give you suggestions for dealing with this issue constructively.

4. *Getting in a rut.* Spiritually speaking, a rut develops when we begin to depend on the method or find security

in the familiar. God quits blessing, and soon the experience of his presence leaves us; however, we continue business as usual. Over time, practicing that pattern conditions us to hold prayer meeting without expecting God's presence or knowing the difference of what it would be like if he were there. As a leader you cannot let yourself fall into this trap. You will constantly need to depend on God to guide the prayer meeting.

Respond from the Heart
(10–15 Minutes)

The purpose of this segment is to allow people to respond to God or continue to prepare their hearts to pray.

I want to give you a challenge. Search the lengthier prayers of the Bible and see how many of them began by asking God for their need. In Nehemiah 9 they prayed twenty-eight verses before asking; in Daniel 9 he prayed twelve verses before stating his request; Solomon reels off thirteen verses before he petitions God in 2 Chronicles 6; Acts 4 records five verses before the church implored God for what they desired; even the Son of God didn't start with a request (see John 17). When you hold up the mirror of this truth to your prayer meeting, what reflection do you see? Unfortunately, the face staring back for most of us is the take-requests/pray-for-them pattern.

If the Son of God didn't even do it in the shadow of the cross and if the apostles didn't do it under threat of persecution, then what makes us think we can when circumstances are far less serious? You will never see God much, if ever, if you start your prayer meeting by praying for your needs.

Let's look at why that is. Think about it from God's perspective. How much of an issue are needs to him? If God were suddenly to exert his great strength by granting every request of all six billion people on earth at once, his reservoir of power would be no more depleted after he did it than before. He has the capacity to solve every problem, silence any hindrance, or fill up any deficiency by a mere snap of his fingers. None of the things we present have escaped his foreknowledge. Before we were created, he already knew, and he can fix them instantaneously. How could any demand placed on an omnipotent, self-sufficient being possibly be of any consequence to him? Would God view cancer, joblessness, or traveling mercies as a fire in the attic that demands suspension of all other considerations until it has been addressed? Of course not; therefore, God doesn't desire prayer meeting to start with needs.

Instead, God starts with his priority. God's primary purpose for prayer is to help his people walk with him. He has determined to work through prayer because it reorients us to him, corrects us when we stray, fans the flames of love, and deepens the intimacy. Where we begin in prayer ought to be where God begins—with the relationship. This frees us to reject the loud, insistent voices of worry demanding that we frantically burst into

God's presence to focus him on our need. Instead we choose to honor him by putting the relationship ahead of the temptation to begin with self. This pleases God, who already knows all about it anyway, and who already knows better than we what to do. When a church loves God so much that its needs become of secondary priority, then the church will see the blessings of God in untold measure. God will give to them in their sleep. Everything they do will turn golden (although not always devoid of trial). Conversely, when a church doesn't love him, they will not find him. In this segment you are allowing people to respond to him in love. Praise, thanksgiving, confession of sin, or a number of other things may be appropriate to renew the relationship with him, but the people must begin with him.

A second reason to begin with God is that we cannot understand what to pray for until our hearts are first rightly related. One of my heroes of the faith is T. W. Hunt, a seasoned saint having walked with God for decades. Over the last forty-five years he has never missed a quiet time, and typically he spends hours in prayer every day with God. I asked him one time to tell me what he does in his time alone with God in the morning. He said, "I set my alarm for 4:00 a.m. Often God wakes me up before then, but if not, I rise when the alarm goes off. Then I begin by meditating on who God is. I realized a long time ago the first reaction every person has to the presence of God was fear, so I meditate on the question, 'Who is God?' until I have a proper awe of who

I'm talking to. Then I read the Bible. Then I praise and thank God. Then I begin interceding for the kingdom and others." As I was doing the math on how much time he spent meditating on who God is, reading his Bible, and praising/thanking God, I blurted out, "T. W., you mean to tell me you spend two hours in the presence of God before you ever ask for a single thing?" He replied, "Well, of course, John. You don't know what to ask until you know who God is."

At the prayer meeting in Acts 4:23–31, the people started off by focusing on God. The response of their heart in verse 29 was to ask for boldness, not protection. Had they not begun with who God is, they surely would have asked for a hedge. You can see what God thought of their prayer meeting in verse 31: "And when they had prayed, the place where they were assembled together was shaken; and they were all filled with the Holy Spirit, and they spoke the word of God with boldness." When the people of God have a heart orientation toward him and not a needs orientation, God moves powerfully in such a way that they experience his answers.

What God Does

During the time of focusing people on God, he will impact hearts. He uses the Scripture, testimony, music, or other means to address the hearts of his people. How he speaks often varies. Some may be stirred toward thanking him, others convicted of sin, and others reminded to trust him. It may vary from prayer meeting to prayer meeting, but you want your people to have the time necessary to respond to him.

While we do not want to program a rigid formula of how God must work, many saints over history have borne witness that thanking God, meditating on his goodness, and remembering his love help prepare them for prayer. Psalm 100 encourages us to "come before His presence with singing . . . be thankful to Him" (vv. 2, 4). Certainly when the people of God are walking with him, this attitude of celebrating his person and presence will be normal. Another standard way of preparing to enter God's presence includes examining one's heart and confessing sin. Most people do better with a repeated pattern; only make sure the pattern doesn't become so rote that the heart disengages.

What a Leader Does

God made you a leader for a reason. People do not naturally know how to relate to God. They must be taught, and they must be reminded. To help people walk in love with God and to respond from their heart, you will practice a minimum of three things:

1. *You will have to coach people on how to relate to God apart from asking what he can give them.* I've led many prayer meetings and have upon occasion given people the specific command not to ask for anything during this segment. They are only allowed to praise and thank him for what he has done. Most people cannot follow those instructions for a full two minutes. So ingrained is the

default response of asking, they can't help themselves. You will have to teach them how to relate to God in ways of thanksgiving and praise. For example, you may want to quote Psalm 100:4, "Enter into His gates with thanksgiving, and into His courts with praise. Be thankful to Him, and bless His name" to show that the normal pattern for coming before God involves a heart response to his goodness. You can lead them to praise and thank God in different ways.

2. *You will have to coach people to pray based on what came to their heart and mind moments earlier.* In the Focus on God section, God will speak to many, but often it's subtle, and they won't recognize it. You will have to train them in making a connection between what they are spiritually understanding and God speaking to them. Then you can guide them to respond to God based on what they are hearing. For example, in seminary I participated in a dynamic prayer group. I didn't know to call what we were doing focusing on God or responding from the heart then, but that's what happened. In this particular group we wanted to eliminate the talking. We began the prayer time by reading aloud, without explanation, Scripture that was on our hearts. After a season of hearing nothing more than the Word of God read, we began praying based on how it impacted us. We would thank God, praise God, confess sin, or meditate on what the verses meant. In this manner of responding, usually the sense of the presence of God would settle. Sometimes one member would begin singing a song on his heart, and

others would join in. By doing this our hearts would be prepared and oriented to God to begin praying more in line with his perspective. In fact, during one two-week stretch we saw more than thirty answers to prayer.

3. *You will have to allow people time to let their hearts respond.* Most Americans are driven to accomplish. The more you pack in, the more you produce. That works for assembly lines but not for relationships. Blistering through an agenda doesn't allow for a heart-to-heart connection. I gave you a one-hour format as a model, but most of the really good prayer meetings I've been in didn't have a set time. I suspect that's because we had all the time we needed to let God speak. Fifteen seconds of silence to let people search their hearts, or two quick lines to say thank you will not build a people who love God. Though this part will be awkward in the beginning for most people, they need to have time to express their hearts to God.

Chapter 5 on activities will give you several ideas for guiding this time.

Seek First the Kingdom
(15–20 minutes)

The purpose of this segment is for people to move onto God's agenda. For people to move onto God's agenda, three things must happen.

1. *They must put God's interests ahead of their own.* Whoever said people are born inherently good must

never have tried to correct the self-centeredness of a two-year-old! In the innocence of that unsophisticated life lies the unmasked, exposed nature we've inherited from Adam. Everything about the little tike perceives the world to revolve around me, my, and mine. Their tiny minds assume they are the center of creation and all other life exists to gratify their desires.

This is the nature received at birth and what we carry through life. Through the infilling of the Holy Spirit and practicing godliness, a Christian can overcome this nature, but it requires constant repetition. Therefore, in your prayer meeting you must quietly make a loud statement by putting this segment ahead of personal needs. You implicitly encourage people to focus on the interests of God ahead of their own. Jesus demonstrated this passion of seeking first his Father and his kingdom in his only recorded boyhood experience. His seedling statement, "I must be about my Father's business," matured into the giant oak of Gethsemane, "Not my will, but yours be done." Jesus, our model, in every way lived a life that sought his Father's interests ahead of his own. As long as we allow our prayer meetings to revolve solely around our needs, or to place our needs first, we cannot expect to be on God's agenda.

2. *The heart priorities of your people must be transformed into God's heart priorities.* Did you know that God doesn't accept a prayer request that is actually his will if the heart of the pray-er has no passion for carrying it out? Too many times we pray the right thing, but it's merely

a matter of the head. In the Bible the phrase *one accord* refers not only to a unified mind but also to a passionate heart. Likewise the phrase "if two or three agree" does not mean that people thought about it for a second, decided it would be a good idea, and therefore they agree to ask for it. Rather it means they jointly so desire what they ask that together they will make any sacrifice God asks of them for it to happen. In Acts 4, when the people requested boldness, their hearts were so inflamed to do the will of God that they willingly embraced the possibility of death in order to see the name of Jesus glorified.

In your prayer meeting God wants to reveal his heart so clearly that it will become his people's heart. When he speaks of the backslidden or the lost, he wants his people to understand the depth of his burden so that it becomes their burden. When the people of God want the will of God to this degree, then we may ask whatever we will, and it shall be done for us. I recently read about Christians in a certain country who are training their people to die. They are sending them as missionaries into parts of the world where certain persecution and death await them. But so passionate are they to see Christ proclaimed that they willingly embrace death. In the 1700s two Moravians became concerned about the souls of slaves in the Caribbean. The only way they knew to reach them was to sell themselves into slavery so that they could work side by side with them. This type of passion can happen for those whose heart priorities have become God's heart priorities.

A simple, 100 percent guaranteed-to-work litmus test will instantly reveal what heart your people have. In your next prayer meeting listen for what is coming out of their mouths (out of the heart the mouth speaks). Do prayer requests for the sick, crises, and other problems dominate, or do people pray for the priorities of God's heart? No one can spend much time in the presence of God without two things becoming their heart—the welfare of the people of God and a desire to impact the world around them. Grief over the backslidden, the spiritual poverty of God's people, the prayerlessness, sin tolerated in Christian's lives, the dying world around them, injustices like girls sold into prostitution slavery in India, and the awful eternity of hell will be the type of staple concerns from those who have heard the heart of God.

3. *The identity of the people of God must be that of a servant to fulfill his desires.* He loves us first, then we learn to love him. As we grow in love, God increasingly reveals his heart to us. In response our identity incorporates his priorities. We become like Jesus, who served with his Father to impact his world. This perhaps more than anything else explains our powerlessness in prayer. When we are not on mission, when we don't know our specific assignment, when we don't know the purpose of God for our lives, then we languish without the experience of God's power.

When those you lead practice Jesus' admonition to "seek first the kingdom of God and His righteousness" (Matt. 6:33), when they put God's priorities ahead of their own, when they see their purpose as being to serve him in their world, then you will see the presence and power of God.

What God Does

God gives his people the same heart that he has. Putting God first is a practice required for the process. Hearing and seeing as God sees gives us the heart he has. Responding and doing this over time forms a life that identifies with his priorities by being on mission.

What a Leader Does

Practically, what do you do?

1. *You must help the people of God wrap their heart around God's heart.* To do this, make prayer requests relational. For example, if you pray for missions, or the backslidden, or the homeless, those are impersonal categories. Jesus, as best I can tell, did not ethereally relate to some ideal called "the masses"; rather, he related to individuals in the crowd. Blind Bartimaeus, the ten lepers, the mute and deaf man, the father with a demon-possessed son, the paralytic, and others were individuals whom he singled out of a crowd to touch. God by nature cannot be impersonal. Too many times we try to stir people based on a category of need instead of helping them encounter actual people to love.

Therefore, if you are going to highlight missions, do it by having a church member from India talk about his lost parents. Have those going on a mission trip to the Appalachian Mountains stand up and let the church pray for them. Let a visiting missionary make an impassioned plea for his place of service.

Speak out of your own passion. If God has not touched your heart, then don't be surprised when no one else's heart is stirred. Passion begets passion. When people catch the sincere fervency you have, then they will more likely be motivated to open their hearts as well. Do not be discouraged that others don't initially share that passion. They haven't walked the same road that you have. Instead be genuinely transparent before them about how God is touching your heart.

Make it visual. It's easier for the heart to embrace what it sees. Show pictures of those in other lands. Hang banners with names of those for whom you are praying. Talk about the lost beside a special cross you have constructed for the occasion. Some gifted communicators can do this with words alone, but for most of us it is easier to have an object that people can see.

2. *Pray in line with how God has been leading you. God does not jump around haphazardly.* Usually he unfolds his will over time. Once he begins in a certain direction, he will continue that way until he has brought it to pass. Therefore, the prayer time should not be disconnected from what you have prayed about in the past. Instead there should be a constant awareness of how to pray

based on reviewing what God has already done. For example, if you are a Sunday school teacher and God has led your class to participate in a foster children's home, then by praying for this every week, you will stay in step with God.

3. *Guide the people of God to discover the will of God together.* There needs to be regular times when you allow people to express what they sense they are hearing from God. By sharing as a group, often the way of God becomes clear. For example, you may want to let participants share Scripture they have read that week or relate stories of God's working in them, or express what has been on their hearts for some time. Knowing what God is doing positions participants to hear from God and secure his power. However, you must first make sure you train your people in knowing when God is speaking to them first.

Present Your Requests
(20–25 minutes)

The purpose of this segment is for God to minister to his people through his people.

I made several disparaging statements about prayer meetings dominated by requests for sickness and crises. Actually, I am not against praying for these things; rather, I'm against prayer meetings characterized by these requests only. Scripture actually commands us to cast all our cares on him and if anyone is sick to call the elders to pray for him. The law of Christ is to bear one another's burdens, and you will naturally pray for those you love. In fact, God himself already wants to touch those who have concerns. Throughout Scripture God blessed, encouraged, and built his people.

In order to guide prayer for sickness, illness, and crises, you must remember two things especially.

1. *Help members see their request from God's perspective.* For example, if someone requests prayer for a loved one in the hospital, you might encourage him to think about why God might have allowed this. Does he want to save a nurse in the process? Is the doctor a Christian who needs strengthening in his faith? What is God teaching the person who is sick? You can ask those questions appropriately and guide people to pray in line with what God is doing.

2. *Mobilize the people of God to minister to one another.* Ephesians 4:12, 16 states that the work of ministry is the edifying of the body of Christ, and that happens when the whole body builds itself up in love as all members do their part. You must never lead and be the whole show. Your job is to set the environment and choose the activities that allow every person to impact one another. Chapter 6 on shepherding will address this in detail.

What God Does

Have you ever had someone pray for you? How did it make you feel? I doubt you came to hate that person, told him to shut up, or felt more alienated from him than ever before. Intuitively, we know that we pray for those we love. When members pray for one another, it builds their love for one another. Have you ever sat down and written out how many of God's answers to prayer came about because you prayed for yourself versus how many came about because someone else prayed for you? I suspect God does most of his work in our lives through the prayers of others. By working in this manner, he causes love for one another to increase.

What a Leader Does

Your job is to guide people in ministering to one another. There are at least four good ways to do this.

1. *Pray for one another in pairs or small groups.* Breaking a large group into smaller groups allows everyone to be prayed for by name. Everyone can give and receive. All participate, and all receive ministry.

2. *Highlight certain individuals with critical or pressing needs.* For example, if someone has heart surgery in the morning, you may mention that to the whole group, then guide all the church to pray for that person.

3. *Guide people to touch one another.* Jesus often touched people as he ministered to them. A hand on a shoulder, kneeling together with an arm around another, or taking someone's hand in prayer communicates concern and encourages a sense of connectedness. This needs to be done appropriately, and considerations of gender and social mores should be taken into consideration. For

example, you don't want men and women kneeling together with their arms around each other unless they're married. Encouraging hand-holding among men creates discomfort for many in our society. Hand-holding with teenagers may create nothing more than an opportunity for flirting. Using wisdom can avert the potholes while capitalizing on a powerful way to minister to one another.

4. *Encourage a close physical proximity.* In other words, when people come to church prayer meeting and sit all over the sanctuary, encourage them to move closer together. If you are in a small group and folks are scattered about the room, have them pull their chairs into a circle. Being closer together gives a greater sense of being connected with one another.

Close in Celebration (5 minutes)

The purpose of this segment is to let people affirm the blessing of having been in God's presence.

Certainly one of the most common attitudes encouraged in prayer is thanksgiving. Paul specifically commanded us to make our requests with thanksgiving (Phil. 4:6; Col. 4:2; 1 Tim. 2:1) and modeled praying that way (Eph. 1:16; Col. 1:3; 1 Thess. 1:2). Little wonder. When a Christian understands that every need of this life is set in the context of canceled sin, regeneration, an eternal inheritance, the presence of the Holy Spirit, being seated with Christ in heavenly places, that we will see God one day as he is, spend eternity with him, and have our mortal bodies resurrected, then how could we do anything else but thank God?

Even if following Christ costs us our life, what is that in comparison to what's awaiting us? Therefore, it is right that we celebrate the privilege of having been in the presence of God, even if the circumstances of life have created pain and heartache. Though our emotions may not always feel it, our spirit can still rejoice in him regardless of the worst circumstances. Bringing closure to a prayer time with celebration is an appropriate way to do that week in and week out. Admittedly, there may be times when God is working something out in hearts due to conviction of sin, or we may be perplexed about something, but normally gratitude and rejoicing ought to be the staple experiences for believers who are right with God and walking with him.

How God Does This

This is more of a time for our response to him in light of what he has done in the prayer meeting. God does it by helping the people recognize his goodness.

How God Uses a Leader

This section need not be long. A leader may make a few encouraging remarks and then guide the people to sing a closing song. Perhaps they can read responsively, or it could be an open-ended time of closure where people break into small groups and praise God, finishing when they sense it is time. The leader's role is to set the parameters of the ending of the prayer meeting and encourage people to express their gratitude to God for hearing and what he will do in response.

The Practice Sheet

You may find it helpful to practice designing a God-centered format at this time. You can review the format proposed in this book on pages 68 and 69. You may practice designing your own format by selecting from the themes given, or you may create your own. In the next chapter we will add the activities to it to give it a greater completeness.

Conclusion

A God-centered format will encourage your people to focus on God's desires, move onto his agenda, and minister to one another. A good format will correct many of the problems in prayer meetings, and it will create a better likelihood that people will encounter God. As a leader you must use this tool well.

Guiding Activities That Involve People

When my two sons were five and three, their sibling rivalry boiled over one day. Conflict resulted replete with all the manifestations of preschoolers with crossed wills. Trying to be a good father, I sat them down and explained that the Bible taught us to edify, to build up one another. About half an hour later my older son had obviously been thinking. "Daddy," he suddenly announced out of the blue, "next time Nathan and I have a fight, I'm going to edify him and not tear him down." I was pleasingly shocked! Teaching that concept to a pre-schooler was difficult at best, but here he was getting it the first time! I enthusiastically responded, "Great son! I'm proud of you! Tell me, how are you going to do that?" He immediately answered in a matter-of-fact voice, "I have no idea."

That reality check to my parenting carries analogies for leading. So many times we know *what* we ought to do but have no clue *how* to do it. Having a good format conceptually organizes where you're going but doesn't provide the handles for steps to take in that direction. That's the function of activities. They put skin on bones. They add color to the picture. They take a concept and make it reality. This chapter will give you multiple, nitty-gritty examples of activities that you could use to lead people in a prayer meeting.

Purpose of Activities

Knowing the purpose of activities guides the practice of activities. You don't want to have people merely jumping through pointless hoops. Activities serve one purpose—to guide people to fulfill God's three desires: responding to his revelation, moving onto his agenda, and ministering to his body through his body. In chapter 3, I listed and defined three broad categories of activities—focusing, participating, and ministering. Focusing activities turn our heart's attention to God or help us see what he's doing. Participating activities guide members to play a part in the prayer meeting. Ministering activities let members build up one another. These three basic strands form the chord of shepherding people in their relationship with God.

Now let's make it even simpler. If I were forced to boil down the three categories of activities to one concept, it would be this: the best way to guide a prayer meeting is to *involve* every person who attends. You want to involve their hearts, their heads, their bodies, their actions, and their leadership. No one can be allowed to be a spectator. Ephesians 4:11–16 and 1 Corinthians 12 explicitly state that every member of the body must be functioning. God has deliberately comprised the body so that all members need the others and that the body builds itself up in love as each member does its part. The focusing, participating, and ministering activities done well will result in the people's being involved.

Unfortunately in many churchwide prayer meetings, people can sit in pews with little required of them. Many leaders, pastors in particular, have unwittingly made a cardinal mistake. They have increasingly assumed a dominating role and have minimized the involvement of those attending. Charles DeWeese traced this historical trend among Baptists. His research concluded that in the 1600–1700s most Baptists did not have trained pastoral leadership. This forced laypeople to be personally responsible to guide meetings for their spiritual well-being. In the 1800s, as Baptists matured, they developed ministers who increasingly began to assume a dominant role that diminished the involvement of the laity. Over the subsequent decades this has produced an inferior quality of disciple.

Oddly enough, the original motivation for the minister to take a greater role stemmed from the recognition that the prayer meeting was critical to church life. Both laity and pastor assumed it couldn't be handled carelessly; instead the most spiritual, the most qualified individual should have responsibility to oversee it. It was a right motivation but a wrong conclusion. It violated the tenor of body life pictured in Scripture. Sitting through an entire service in a pew while watching one person do everything is not what God intended. Instead the leader should be a facilitator of the meeting, not a dominator.

Activities that involve are how you do that. Focusing activities primarily involve the heart. Participating activities involve all attending, require their leadership, and require their bodies to move (which makes them more likely to participate). Ministering activities involve everyone in building up one another. If we allow people just to sit, they will be less likely to see God, their growth will be slowed, and many people in prayer meeting will leave with unmet needs.

Discussion of each type of activity and multiple examples of what could be done follow. As you read, keep three things in mind. First, the lists are not exhaustive, and God may guide you to do other things as well. Second, any of the three activities could be used at any point in the format. Third, many activities overlap. For example, if you take testimonies from the floor, that is both a focusing activity and a participating activity. If you have people gather around someone to pray, that is both a ministering and a participating activity. Defining which category an activity fits matters little; rather, seek to do what best shepherds your people.

Focusing Activities

A focusing activity may be defined as any activity that focuses the people on God or helps them see what he is doing. The most common examples are singing, testifying, and reading Scripture.

The primary purpose of focusing activities is to orient participants to God by setting or maintaining the focus on him. People's hearts tend to drift and need to recognize what God is doing or simply to come into one accord. An indispensable leadership function is to focus people in the right direction.

Who does the activities? The leader has the ultimate responsibility to make sure this happens. He can do this personally through the words he says, the use of Scripture, or a visual demonstration. Additionally, he can set the focus by guiding participants to give a testimony, share a word from the Lord, or use video or drama. He will enlist people ahead of time and/or encourage participation from those attending.

These activities are best used at the beginning of the prayer meeting in the focus-on-God segment and at times of transition between prayer sets.

Examples of Ways to Focus People on God

Scripture

- Read a passage and expound on it. This is the most common way practiced in churches today. For example, you could expound from Psalm 139 that the Lord especially acquaints himself with our ways (v. 3). That's why David prayed, "See if there is any wicked way in me" (v. 24). He is a God who examines our ways, our lifestyles. What are your ways?

- Have different people read assigned verses on a particular theme. For example, if you could have people read about the greatness of God, you could assign Isaiah 40:12–17; 42:9–12; 43:9–13; 45:5–8.

- Have three or more people read a verse or passage from different translations. Let them meditate on what struck them after each reading, then lead them to pray.

- Let different people share favorite verses of their choosing. For example, you could set the stage by asking, "What has God done for you? Can you give a verse that captured a significant moment when God came and worked in your life?"

- Let people read verses that have spoken to them that week. This helps them pay attention to God's current activity.

- Give a specific verse and have people tell how they have seen God work it out in their lives.
- Have people write letters to God in response to a particular verse of Scripture.

Testimony

- Preassign a testimony based on what God did in someone's life that week. For example, if God made an obvious financial provision for someone that week, have him or her tell about it.
- Recruit a few people ahead of time or ask from the floor for people to give one-minute testimonies. This controls excessive talking, involves more people, and gives a bigger picture of what God is doing in the church body.
- Take testimonies from a large group of what God has done that week in people's lives.
- Break into small groups and let members share what God has done that week. This is great in a church where God is working among the majority. If most members don't have a testimony, it will create awkwardness.

Music

- Encourage participants to sing from their hearts. Inject intention. Comment briefly on the meaning of the song to be sung. Memorize words and make eye contact with the audience.

- Choose several songs with a thematic message. For example, on redemption you could sing "There Is a Fountain Filled with Blood," "Nothing but the Blood of Jesus," and "Are You Washed in the Blood?"
- Play the same song in different ways to communicate nuances of our relationship with God— softly, majestically, insistently, celebratively, relaxed. For example, play "Amazing Grace."
- Stop in the middle of a song and have people pray, then sing the rest of the song. For example, sing "God Is So Good," take testimonies, then sing it again. Also see Psalm 136.
- Play a familiar song instrumentally to help people reflect on what it means. For example, play "People Need the Lord" in the background while getting ready to pray for the lost, or while praying for the lost.
- Take requests for songs that are based on Scripture.
- Take song requests from participants and have each person tell why the song helps him connect with God. For example, if someone asks to sing "In the Garden," he could describe how he learned to get up early and be alone with the Lord and the sweetness of that fellowship.
- Use one song repetitively as a theme after prayer sets. For example, at a spiritual awakening

conference, throughout the week you could sing a theme song on brokenness.

Video

- Flash a PowerPoint collage of Scripture on the screen. This is a variation of doing Scripture thematically.
- Videotape a testimony and play the video. This could be a testimony from someone outside the congregation, or by a member who is absent. Sometimes the stories may be better communicated through editing.
- Use nature scenes to accompany worship. This can be a support to music. You can find professional companies that produce material for this purpose.

Drama

- Act out a skit.
- Dramatize Scripture that was just read.

Visual Objects

You can use a number of props that support what you are talking about. For example:

- Carry a baby in your arms and talk about God as Father.
- Hold up a globe. Talk about the God of Genesis 1:1 who created this world and is the same God

of Psalm 2:8 who is giving the world to his Son. Lead prayer for missions.

- Set up a cross to focus people on sacrifice, or pray for the lost, or remind the people how much God loves them.
- Use banners. One church made several banners with various prayer themes such as believers, ministries, the lost, government officials, schools, and family. Then they broke their people into small groups and had them pray five to ten minutes at each station. At the appropriate signal, the groups rotated to pray at the next banner.
- Use posters/large sheets in the same way banners are used.

Small Objects

Giving people an object to hold tangibly helps many people focus more easily. If it can be carried home, it can be a reminder throughout the week. For example:

- Hand out a small rock and speak about how God is our rock.
- Hand out candles or matches or flashlights to speak about God as light. Read appropriate text.
- Hand out keys and talk about God as a door.
- Use objects to talk about God as bread, the vine, Alpha and Omega (A to Z), the branch, shield, or fortress.

Physical Location

The environment of the room can set a subtle influence on focusing people on God.

- Turning the lights down low sets a reflective mood.
- With the lights low, a spotlight can be shown onstage with no one in it. If the leader is off-stage using a microphone, it allows the prayer meeting to be guided, but no human figure is seen—only a spotlight with no one in it. The effect helps focus people on God, not man.
- Pray in the shell of the new sanctuary. This special service for dedicating a new building to God helps people see what could be. You could similarly pray in the Sunday school room where a new class is being launched.
- Prayer-walking or praying on site draws attention to a particular place or concern. For example, if elections are coming up, you could go and pray at your local government building. If you want to reach a particular neighborhood, you could organize teams to walk through it while praying over it.
- Praying from the top of a mountain or a tall building over the city below—getting a bird's-eye view from up high—often helps people get a sense of one of the ways God views their city.
- Circle the sanctuary and pray for Sunday services.

Words

How you say things will set the focus as well. Speak in a way that focuses people's minds and hearts.

- Ask questions—particularly questions that make people think, that probe the heart. For example: "When was the last time you experienced a fresh touch from God? On a scale of 1 to 10 what is your passion level? Do you really expect God to answer you, or are you just going through an exercise called prayer?"
- Offer reminders. State the obvious, what people already know. For example, "Now, you remember that Paul said God would do immeasurably more than all we ask or think. Is that true? Would that apply right now?"
- Use declarative statements. Affirming the truth refocuses us as well. A number of years ago, the pastor in my church would regularly say, "God is good!" and the people would respond, "All the time!" Then he would say, "All the time," and the people would declare, "God is good."

Printed Material, Acronyms, or Catchy Phrases

- Read well-written material.
- Go over a sin list.
- Use ABCs to praise God by having an attribute that begins with each letter.

- Use the ACTS acrostic, which stands for adoration, confession, thanksgiving, supplication. You may guide people to pray following this model.
- Use the word PRAY as an acrostic. This stands for praise, repent, adore, and yield.
- Use ASK as an acrostic. Matthew 7:7 says to ask, seek, and knock. Lead people to ASK by praying intensely in line with Matthew 7:7.

A Function Unique to Focusing Activities

Focusing activities will be a staple to make the transition between prayer sets. When you are about to conclude one time of prayer and introduce the next, you must set the focus in such a way that God is preeminent and hearts come into one accord. Here are some pointers in making the transitions between prayer sets.

1. Catch them before the praying goes flat. When people are in prayer sets, don't wait until every group has finished praying. You can make the transition at any time, but when two-thirds of the people are finished praying, it's definitely time to move to another prayer set.

2. Use music to cue people to be winding down. One way you alert people to wrap up their prayers is by having an instrumentalist begin playing softly in the background. After a few seconds, you can begin moving them to the next prayer set.

3. If you have no music, you can close by giving a
    verbal alert or by praying. You say something
    like, "We'll take another minute," or you may
    simply begin praying above everyone else.

4. If there is a spirit of prayer, your transition times
    will usually be short. Say just enough to intro-
    duce the next prayer set and topic, then pray. As
    a rule your words or a Scripture verse will be sta-
    ples. Quoting a verse or reminding what the
    Bible says is usually sufficient to direct it.

5. Occasionally transitions will take time. You may
    use any number of activities to focus people on
    God.

Participating Activities

A participating activity is any activity that requires
participation of the heart, the head, the body, and leadership. The most common examples are small groups,
singing, and sharing leadership.

The primary purpose of participating activities is to
involve all attendees in responding to God, both numerically and physically. According to Ephesians 4:11–12,
God did not call the leader to do the work of ministry.
He called the leader to equip the people of God to do the
work of ministry. You must create activities that allow all
the people to play a part. The best way to create participation is to involve as many people as you can both
numerically and physically.

Who does the activities? The leader has the ultimate responsibility to facilitate them, but the *people* are the ones who must carry them out.

These activities may occur at any time.

Examples of Participation Activities

Numerical

You want as many people as possible to participate. Here are examples of ways to involve various people in leading or participating.

- Assign different people to lead prayer sets.
- Recruit a volunteer to read a Scripture passage.
- Sing hymns and choruses.
- Break into small groups.
- Use testimonies.
- In large groups use sentence prayers.
- Use responsive readings.
- Have everyone praying all at once out loud. First, the leader announces the topic to be prayed for, then encourages everyone to pray. Some people like this; some do not. Know your group.
- Plan prayer walks.
- Swap names of lost people. People can write the name of a lost person on a slip of paper, then swap with someone else in the congregation.
- Organize cell phone praying. A member calls someone in need of prayer, then a small group or large group prays for that person.

- Plan ways for participants to join together. Have people pray individually; then in the next prayer time have them pray in pairs. Then have two pairs join together; then have those two pairs join with two other pairs and so on until the entire group is united.

Physical

People's bodily participation often encourages their hearts to participate. Here are examples of ways to engage their bodies.

- Stand and sing.
- Form small groups. When people break into small groups, they must turn their bodies toward one another.
- Kneel to pray. Kneeling is the posture most representative of humility and submission.
- Write a prayer card. Have members write a prayer card to individuals in need of prayer.
- Clasp hands. Encourage people to take the hands of those in their small group or another individual they are praying with.
- Join hands across the aisle.
- Pray with your hand on the shoulder of the person in front of you.
- Stand to pray with another. Standing communicates readiness. Having people stand to pray with another often makes it easier for them to pray in expectation.

- Come to the altar. Ask people to leave their seats and come forward to seek God.
- Cup hands together. Another way to communicate expectation is to put your hands together, as if expecting to receive something from God.
- Rotate banners. People must walk from one banner to the next to pray for the topic of the banner.
- Focus prayer through prayer-walking.
- Move to surround a member in need of prayer.
- Place hands on a person to pray. This of course requires people to move bodily and ministers to the one being prayed for.
- Have people stretch out their hands to the person being prayed for. This is best used when the group is large and it's awkward to try to surround another believer. Instead they can "reach out" by extending their arms toward the person and praying.
- Pray on one's face or hands and knees, stretching out.
- Pray with arms raised to heaven.

Ministering Activities

A ministering activity is one that leads people to minister to one another. The primary purpose is for the body to minister to and build itself up in love. According to Ephesians 4:11–16, God gave ministers to equip the saints to build up the body, and as each part does its job, the body builds itself up in love. Prayer meetings provide a rich opportunity to do just that.

Who does the activities? The leader has the responsibility to facilitate them, but the *people* are the ones who carry them out. They may occur at any time, but more often than not you will use them in the segment of the format when kingdom and personal requests are presented.

Examples of Ministering Activities

Here are some examples of ways to minister to one another in prayer.

- Pray for one another by name. Have people break into pairs or small groups to do this.
- Highlight special groups, such as new mothers, high school students, those with cancer, or those going on a mission trip. Have a special time in the prayer meeting to minister to them by lifting them up in prayer.
- Use a prayer chair. Have those needing prayer sit in a prayer chair. Each time someone sits in it, the others pray for the person. In smaller groups the chair should be set in the middle of the group. In a larger group the chair may be placed facing the auditorium, and those leading will stand behind the person to pray.
- Bless one another. Break into pairs or small groups. Lead members to tell God specifically

why they are thankful for the person or people
they are praying with. A variation is to do this as
a large group.

- Go find three friends and tell them why you
thank God for them. This is a variation of blessing one another. The major difference is it creates more movement and usually is a little easier
for people to do.

- Kneel beside one another at the altar. Ask other
participants to come alongside those at the altar,
or in their seats, with burdens and pray with
them. Usually it's a good idea for women to
pray with women and men with men.

- Place a hand on a shoulder to pray. Often the
power of touch ministers.

- Write prayer cards. Have all participants write a
prayer for an individual. Collect prayer cards and
mail them to the person prayed for. Knowing
they are loved will encourage that person.

- Open a time taking one or two requests, then
praying for them. After taking one or two
requests, stop and pray for the requests just
given.

- Use the one-dollar blessing. Have everyone pray
for an individual or group and give one dollar to
him.

- Use the pager blessing. Get the pager number
of the person to be prayed for ahead of time.
Every time a member prays have him page the

person and enter #123. This will alert them that they have just been prayed for.

- Anoint with oil. Sometimes people who are sick desire this to be done for them. It is a way to minister to the individual.

Conclusion

Activities are practical ways to shepherd. You shepherd according to God's three great desires—revealing himself to his people, moving them onto his agenda, and ministering to his people. You know those you lead and what works best with them. Choose activities that fit your context.

CHAPTER 6

Shepherding the People of God

The Importance of Shepherding

A name communicates the essence of a person. For example, when you read the name *Adolf Hitler,* what immediately comes to mind? If I write *Michaelangelo,* what do you think about? If you hear the name *Billy Graham,* what kind of a man do you envision? A name sums up, it characterizes a person—how he functions, what he is like, what he does. When Scripture ascribes a name to God, it pictures a fundamental essence of his being. Any time God reveals a name describing his character, it carries tremendous importance, precisely because it was chosen. Here's what I mean. If God is infinite, how many names could he have? It would stand to reason he has as many names as the size of his person. The few hundred revealed in the Bible would be like selecting a few hundred grains of sand from among the sand on the seashore. Therefore, when Scripture selects a name from the vast possibilities, it is important. Just think, then, how important it is when God calls himself by a certain name multiple times.

One of those oft-repeated names is Shepherd. To give you an idea of its frequency, Scripture calls Jesus Savior sixteen times and Shepherd twelve times. He is the Shepherd (Matt. 26:31), the good Shepherd (John 10:11), great Shepherd (Heb. 13:20), the Shepherd and Overseer of your souls (1 Pet. 2:25), and the Chief Shepherd (1 Pet. 5:4). The name takes a seat at the table as one of the seven "I Am" statements in John. Not surprisingly, God's explicit self-stated desire is to shepherd his people (Jer. 23:4; Ezek. 34:12), and the Bible refers to him shepherding his people more than thirty times. He requires his leaders to function as shepherd nearly forty times. Some of the harshest judgments in the Bible were pronounced against bad shepherds (Jer. 25; Ezek. 34), whereas those who served well as shepherds were commended in the most glowing terms. A bedrock prophecy of the Messiah was that he would shepherd the sheep others had driven away (Ezek. 34:16–23). Do you see the importance of this name? Do you see the frequency and intensity with which God reveals himself by this title? Anyone wishing to grasp the nature of God must include understanding him as shepherd.

Your People Need Shepherding

If God is a shepherd, he must have sheep, which would be us. If you've ever cared for sheep, you know being called one is not necessarily a compliment. My grandfather raised sheep in the hills of northern Kentucky. If his sheep laid down on an incline pointing uphill, they were so helpless they couldn't get their legs under them to stand up again. Then they would die within twenty-four hours!

I heard another story about sheep in Ireland huddling for warmth in the corner of rock fences when the north wind blows. After a while they eat all the grass, but because of the cold, they refuse to move on to other pasture. When their hunger intensifies, they eat the wool off one another, which results in many of them freezing to death.

Another story involved a shepherd with a split-rail corral. In order to get the sheep out in the morning, he would remove the top rail and prod the sheep until the first one jumped over the remaining bottom rail. Since sheep imitate one another's behavior, the rest would follow suit. One day while they were jumping, he decided to experiment by removing the bottom rail also. Although they could now walk out, each sheep continued mindlessly to jump at the spot of the nonexistent rail.

Additional stories of inabilities include being unable to drink from a running stream, straying, giving up when attacked, and susceptibility to disease. Being called a sheep is no compliment if judged on the basis of intelligence and self-sufficiency.

Why would God name us that? Putting ego aside, sheep more than any other animal embody key dynamics in our relationship with God. They must have the constant oversight of the shepherd's care guarding, leading, and feeding. On their own sheep are prone to wander, scatter, self-destruct, and are defenseless against predators. Sheep thrive only when they have a shepherd. Similarly, we are dependent on the watchcare of God. It doesn't take much for our heart to wander in our spiritual life, and left to our own devices, we would be easy prey for Satan's deceptions. Without the constant care and leadership of the Lord, we would perish.

God is the great Shepherd and certainly could do the shepherding by himself. However, 1 Peter 5:1–4 pictures Christ as a ruling shepherd who has appointed others to serve him as undershepherds. Without controversy this passage teaches that if you are a pastor, you must see your role as that of shepherd. Personally, I believe this principle also extends to any leader in church life with positions impacting the spiritual walk of others. If you serve as a staff member, an elder or deacon, or lead a Sunday school class, you are a shepherd over that group. On a scale of one to ten, the importance of this requirement for you is an eleven. Just how important may be seen from five biblical references. John closes his Gospel by dedicating the entire final chapter to Jesus' charge to Peter to shepherd his sheep. When God commanded Moses to ascend the mount to die, the first words out of his mouth upon hearing this were, "Let the LORD, the God of the spirits of all flesh, set a man over the congregation, who may go out before them and go in before them, who may lead them out and bring them in, that the congregation of the LORD may not be like sheep which have no shepherd" (Num. 27:16–17). The people who anointed David king understood that leaders must shepherd, saying, "Also, in time past, when Saul was king over us, you were the one who led Israel out and brought them in; and the LORD said to you, 'You shall shepherd My people Israel, and be ruler over Israel'" (2 Sam. 5:2).

In two negative examples God declares blistering judgment against those who abuse this charge:

"Therefore, you shepherds, hear the word of the LORD: 'as I live,' says the Lord GOD, 'surely because My flock became a prey, and My flock became food for every beast of the field, because there was no shepherd, nor did My shepherds search for My flock, but the shepherds fed themselves and did not feed My flock'— therefore, O shepherds, hear the word of the LORD! Thus says the Lord GOD: 'Behold, I am against the shepherds, and I will require My flock at their hand; I will cause them to cease feeding the sheep, and the shepherds shall feed

themselves no more; for I will deliver My flock
from their mouths, that they may no longer be
food for them.'" (Ezek. 34:7–10)

"Woe to the worthless shepherd,
Who leaves the flock!
A sword shall be against his arm
And against his right eye;
His arm shall completely wither,
And his right eye shall be totally blinded."
(Zech. 11:17)

Your people need a shepherd, and shepherding is
important stuff! If you lead a group or church, it ought
to be with fear and trembling. Your leadership will be
judged or rewarded based on how well you have fulfilled
this assignment. The seriousness of it begs the question,
What is it, and how do I do it?

What Is Shepherding?

As always, the best place to start is with Jesus. What
does the Scripture picture him doing? One of the passages that succinctly sums up his pattern of ministry
occurs in Matthew 9:35–38:

Jesus went about all the cities and villages,
teaching in their synagogues, preaching the
gospel of the kingdom, and healing every sickness and every disease among the people. But
when He saw the multitudes, He was moved
with compassion for them, because they were

weary and scattered, like sheep having no shepherd. Then He said to His disciples, "The harvest truly is plentiful, but the laborers are few.
Therefore pray the Lord of the harvest to send
out laborers into His harvest."

Jesus saw a shepherdless people. He responded in
four ways.

1. He taught them the relationship with God in
   their synagogues (v. 35).
2. He sought to move people onto God's agenda
   through preaching the good news of the kingdom (v. 35).
3. He ministered to their needs through healing
   sickness or disease (v. 35).
4. He spoke out of his heart to the hearts of the
   disciples to stir their hearts. He was moved with
   compassion; therefore, he spoke to his disciples
   from and for that same passion (vv. 36–38).

Jesus fulfilled the desires of God for his people.
He showed how to relate to God, drew back those
wandering on the mountains of their own agenda, and
restored others' souls. As he practiced these things, he
was training the disciples to be like him. (He sent them
out in chapter 10 to do the same things he had done.)
His words were spoken to their hearts in a way that
stirred them to action. These four practices of shepherding can be summarized into one idea. *The defini-
tion of shepherding is leading the people of God to walk with
God.*

That's what you must do. You must shepherd the people of God in such a way that they walk with him. They should be growing in their relationship with him, increasingly seeking first his kingdom, and fervently ministering to one another. The passion of your heart will speak to theirs to stir them in this direction. If you are fulfilling this assignment, there will be evidence. Here are seven questions to evaluate whether God is using you to shepherd his people:

- Do my people have a passionate, growing love for God?
- Do my people act and think more like Jesus than they once did?
- When they go to pray in their prayer closet, are they praying any differently based on what they learned from prayer meeting?
- Is God responding to prayers by giving my church or small group greater opportunities for kingdom service? Am I seeing doors opening to be involved in his work?
- Is there greater evidence of God's activity in our prayer meeting because my people are changing to focus more on his desires?
- Is their love for one another growing? Do they have an increasing heart for ministering to one another? Do I see their koinonia deepening? Does their love drive them to persevere in prayer for one another?

- Can people divorce, fall away, or walk out of
  the church without the lights burning longer in
  the prayer meeting? Do people take action after
  the prayer meeting to restore straying members?

These questions ask about results. They give insight as to how well you are doing the *what* of shepherding, but they don't tell you how to do it. They beg the question, Practically, how do I shepherd, particularly in prayer?

What Do You Do and Why?

Shepherding is an art, not a science. It's one thing to describe shooting a basketball; it's another to communicate in words the fluidity, the feel, the intuition, the art of it. To do this let's look at shepherding as it relates to the material of the other chapters. You will notice overlap, but hopefully it will better connect the dots on how to use the tools we've discussed earlier. Some examples illustrate the concepts.

Listed below are five tools for shepherding:

1. *Integrity in living out what you call for.* You are the visible example. God chooses a leader whom he has impacted to impact his people. A leader who knows God leads other people to know God. A person of prayer begets people of prayer. This means you must know God intimately. No one can teach beyond what he knows. Leaders can't move people onto an agenda they're not on themselves. They can't lead people to minister to others

if they don't set the pace. You can't fake this if you don't live it. Polish or professionalism without integrity won't produce anything. So much of what people learn springs from seeing a visible demonstration of a godly life. I've already said this several times earlier in the book, and it should go without saying, but I say it again to reiterate its importance.

2. *The attitude of shepherding.* You must have the identity of a shepherd. You should walk in the prayer meeting with an attitude of being a servant of God, thinking, *My reason for existence is to please him, to do his will. I am coming with my church/small group to seek his face. I bear responsibility to guide that process so that hearts are ready to hear and respond to him. I recognize that much of his working will be what he is doing in his people. I need to pay attention to how lives are being impacted as much as I do to the actual requests being prayed. I need to be ready to respond based on what best helps them become all that God has in mind.* Too many prayer meetings have no greater purpose than to pray for requests and to teach the Bible. This wasted opportunity for leading people to walk with God stems from lacking the identity of a shepherd.

3. *The format you choose.* Shepherds often create structure that allows them to do their job. A corral is a boundary that sets the parameters for the sheep. It keeps them from wandering and helps them stay in one accord. Similarly the format structures the prayer time so that people don't wander and they stay together on the same page. It schedules the blocks of learning the relationship

with God, moving onto his agenda, and ministering to one another. Chapter 4 offers a recommended format and how to use it.

4. *The activities you use.* Psalm 143:10 says, "Teach me to do Your will." The Great Commission states, "Teaching them to observe all things that I have commanded you" (Matt. 28:20). Luke 11:1 reads, "Lord, teach us to pray." In all three cases the request is for a lifestyle practice. They do not cry for a mental understanding alone. In the twentieth and twenty-first centuries, the word *teach* has come to mean the transfer of information from instructor to pupil. The job of a teacher is to distill a body of information into a presentable form so that the learner may master it. When that happens, we call it learning. Not so in the Bible. The word *teach* primarily relates to the character development of the student. The Bible only considers a disciple to have learned when he practices a biblical command. No one has taught the Bible until their hearers do what it says. You cannot call yourself a teacher by explaining the Great Commandment, clarifying the Sermon on the Mount, or shedding light on the love chapter. You may only call yourself a teacher when your students practice what Scripture advocates.

Why is that? Why does the Bible take this approach? The answer lies in understanding how God designed for us to learn the relationship with him. If I want to learn about cooking, I read a book. If I want to learn to cook, I must cook. If I want to know God, it does not happen because I read what the Bible says. It happens because I obey what the Bible says. Jesus led the disciples to know him by involving them in his work, not by sermons alone. In Matthew 10, he sent the Twelve out on their first mission trip even before Peter had made his great confession. However, as they did the will of God, they came to know more about him. Upon the return of the seventy, they exclaimed a new understanding, "Lord, even the demons are subject to us in your name" (Luke 10:17). Walking with him over three years prepared them to understand what he wanted in Acts. Through involving them in his ministry, he shepherded them to learn the relationship with God.

Activities, more than anything else, are the way you do that in prayer meeting. They model, mobilize, and mold lives into the practices that God desires. An old saying goes, "Tell me and I will forget, show me and I will remember, involve me and I will be changed for a lifetime." When you facilitate activities that demonstrate how to walk with God, your people will internalize the life Christ intends. Let's take the three types of activities and explain how they shepherd:

Focusing. If you have people read the Word of God, share what God has done that week in their lives, or explain how they came to recognize God's speaking from Scripture, you set a pattern for their private prayer life. Among beginners, they almost always pray privately according to what they've experienced publicly. Beginners rarely have clear ideas of how to put concepts into practice on their own but can easily imitate what they see modeled. Thus you teach the relationship with God, how to get in a position to hear him, how to recognize his voice, and how to discipline oneself not to be distracted in life.

Participating. Facilitating people to do what they are learning has at least two benefits. First, these activities create platforms for people to practice what they are learning from God. By exercising themselves, they learn the habits of godliness. Second, when you involve some-one, his heart more readily wraps around the things of God. Matthew 6:21–24 teaches that the heart ultimately clings to what it treasures and serves. Prayer cannot be practiced as a passive exercise. All the great prayer warriors in the Bible were men and women of action. Abraham, Moses, Elijah, David, Paul, and Jesus did not pray and sit. They acted. They seized the day. They boldly did something. Prayer will lead to acting regard-ing what you pray about. People will most likely move onto God's agenda when they do God's agenda. They develop a heart to minister to others by ministering to others. Therefore, you want to involve people in doing the will of God in prayer meeting.

Ministering. Jesus said the one defining mark of his followers would be: "By this all will know that you are My disciples, if you have love one for another" (John 13:35). Prayer creates an incredible opportunity for the people of God to love, minister to, and bear one another's burdens. When you lead people to surround a member of the body who is hurting, take up a collection for someone in financial need, or write prayer cards to a victim of cancer, your people learn to show love to their brother and sister. You teach them a lifestyle of loving their neighbor as themselves. In the church I currently pastor, increasing this practice has had more impact on raising the level of prayer than anything else I've done. Recently in a prayer meeting at my church, we spent time thanking God for the people in our church (like Paul in Phil. 1:3–4). We did this by going to two or three people and telling them why we thanked God for them. Tears were on several faces, and everyone was edified. By practicing building one another up, the tone of the prayer meetings was greatly animated. Several people there needed that touch from the Lord. This activity modeled how to build one another up with the tongue in everyday life.

5. *The words you say.* First Corinthians 14:1 tells which spiritual gift we ought to desire above the rest—prophecy. Verse 3 explains why—those who prophesy speak to edify, encourage, and console the church. Paul spends the next thirty-seven verses to make only one point. Whatever you do in church, especially seek to edify your brother. He viewed the ability to speak words to the heart that spiritually impact the hearers as the greatest spiritual gift one could desire. Powerful words are the equivalent of a shepherd's rod and staff. Ecclesiastes 12:11 says, "The words of the wise are like goads, and the words of scholars are like well-driven nails, given by one Shepherd." A spiritual shepherd uses

words to goad or build. If you are a leader, the words you say will have as much impact as any other single thing you do. In order to speak to shepherd, you must know where and how to aim your words.

Target the heart. Don't talk for information; talk for transformation. Jesus left no sermon at the factual level only, no dispassionate discourse on the mechanics of kingdom principles. Instead he understood the secret of seizing his listeners by the heart so that they were compelled to respond. That response proved favorable in some; in others it led to his crucifixion; but none were left unaffected. In Acts 2:37 Peter's sermon "cut to the heart." In Acts 7:54 Stephen's sermon "cut to the heart." Jesus, Peter, and Stephen understood how to access the internal workings of a man, how to finger the right heart button for action, or dig up the reoccurring weeds of errant motives, thoughts, and desires that creep back into our hearts. They did not dabble in merely transferring information to the head but spoke to the heart. They understood that out of the heart spring the issues of life (Prov. 4:23).

Many people leading prayer meetings speak merely to the head. I'm not against speaking to the head. We need to have knowledge, but knowledge alone does not lead people to respond to God. They must stand up on the inside before they can walk with God on the outside. They must internalize, they must wrap their heart around the things of God before they will do the will of God. You cannot just go over a prayer list or work through a sermon. You must know where you want the people to go in their relationship with God.

Today in all the Christian talk on leadership, I especially fear. So much is made of method and technique and so little of speaking to the souls of men. I wonder at times if a subtle perversion hasn't taken place. Recognizing the benefits of strategy, administration, and organization, conferencing on leadership locks in on these topics. The tendrils of an insidious danger have imperceptibly begun to wind themselves around us. Oddly enough these pernicious shoots don't stem from a lie but from the truth. It is true that improved methods in these arenas will help. But somehow the old man that's resident within each of us, laden with pride and desire, can easily seize upon that which is good and turn it toward a corrupted end. We may misplace our confidence in these things for success rather than a transformed heart, until that which was once pure becomes impure. Then we put the priority on leadership techniques for success. If we speak primarily at the mechanical, organizational, program, or goals level, a creeping ivy of spiritual complacency will wrap around the souls of our people; their garden will choke with weeds; and the fruit of spiritual vibrancy will be stunted. Therefore, one of the preeminent jobs of shepherding is to speak to the hearts of your followers.

In prayer meeting you will do that in three arenas especially: when you set the focus on God, when you make transitions from prayer set to prayer set, and when you are overseeing ministering activities. Here are some examples of what I mean.

- If you are going to pray for the lost, don't say, "Now let's pray for kingdom requests. We've got to make a difference in this world." Instead focus people on God's heart and their responsibility. Say something like, "What is the heart of God? When you draw near to him, what do you hear him saying about what he sees? Do you have the dread reality of hell before you? Can you see that person in the final outcome? When was the last time you tasted the salt of your tears for souls?"

- If you are transitioning, don't say, "Next we will pray for the sick." Instead say, "Some among us need a fresh touch from the Lord. The Bible says the Lord cares, therefore we care. Let's lift up our brothers and our sisters right now. Will your heart pray for them as much as God's heart desires their burdens to be cast upon him?"

- If you are leading a ministering activity of praying for someone, don't say, "We're supposed to pray for one another. Let's do that right now and pray for Sam." Instead say, "We appreciate Sam so much. Think of the times he has blessed you. Now it's our turn to bless him. Let's lift our brother, whom we love, up to the Lord right now."

Speak for understanding. Show how God thinks, what his ways are. Jesus sought to change the understanding of the disciples. We are transformed by the renewing of our minds. Over 40 percent of Paul's intercessory prayers requested that God would impact the understanding of his followers. Your hearers must understand why they do what they do in prayer meeting. As a leader you will have multiple opportunities to interpret how to pray, what answers to prayer mean, what pleases God, and what he likes or dislikes. You will often preface a prayer time with a brief, one-to-five-minute explanation of something about God.

For example, a participant says, "I have a praise! You remember when we prayed I would get a job last week? Two days later it happened, and it pays better than the old one!" At that moment you may say any number of things God lays on your heart, such as, "Do you realize what just happened? God cannot answer your prayer request without answering you. Your God just drew alongside of you at your cry and personally gave you a job because he personally was loving you." Or you may want to say, "Church, do you see how God responded when we prayed in faith? We had been praying before based on the need, but when we prayed in faith, God immediately answered."

People need help in praying for the sick and those in crisis. You will want to remind them to cry out to God in expectation and refocus them on what God may be doing. For example, when a member goes to the hospital, you may gently remind the people that God already knew of this day before it happened. You may then ask, "What might God want to do with Lisa's life? Are there nurses and doctors he wants to touch? Are there others who need inspiration from her example?" Paul taught the Philippians how to watch and pray. In Philippians 1:12–19 he taught them how to interpret the selfish ambitions of others, and the trouble he personally received. He was shepherding them to know how to respond.

Speak for passion. Scripture teaches, "The effective, *fervent* prayer of a righteous man avails much" (James 5:16). You cannot merely go over a list and expect to avail much. Walk through the Bible and pause at the answers to prayer. Notice how many times sincere desire or crying out precedes God's response. People grow in fervency if passion speaks to passion. Your sincere desire must be present to stir sincere desire in others. You cannot let the cares of this world, the desire for other things, and the deceitfulness of riches choke it out. Do not try to manufacture or manipulate passion, but if your heart is sincere, people will usually respond.

Here's an example of stirring passion. Read Isaiah 26:9, "With my soul I have desired You in the night, yes, by my spirit within me I will seek You early." Talk about intensity! Expound on how Isaiah rose in the night because he was so hungry for God. Ask, "Have you ever been that hungry before? What about when you were first saved? Or was there a season of crisis when God drew near and your heart leaped even though it carried a weight of grief? Have you ever known that hunger? How hungry are you now? This is a question I've been asking of myself lately. Might I ask it of you? Felicia, when was the last time you got up at midnight because you so hungered to know God? John, have you this past week set the alarm clock back a little to get up early and seek God? Melinda, when did you last set aside time to do nothing but read the Bible? Did the pages seem to come alive because God was pouring out living water on the desire of your thirsty soul? Let's seek him right now. Let's go to him in prayer and ask him to renew a passion for him in each of us."

Speak for encouragement. People respond to positive motivation better than negative motivation. By requesting, inviting, exhorting, and urging, you will more likely strengthen their willingness. Whenever possible ask—don't tell. For example, if you are leading the church or small group to pray for someone, you may encourage people to pray with statements such as, "Would you mind surrounding Paul right now?" Other times you may want to invite with statements like, "If you feel led, kneel where you are and voice a prayer to the Lord."

Speak for conviction. We all have trouble in prayer because our minds drift. How easily we seize upon some worldly pleasure until it seizes us. For Christians this often is done unintentionally. We experience some good gift from the hand of God and rejoice in the benefit it brings, but having experienced its pleasure, we begin to lose focus and seek the gift instead of the Giver. Or

perhaps we allow comfort or complacency to inch their
way imperceptibly into our lives until we suddenly find
ourselves resisting a call to sacrifice. These shifting
desires are at work in each heart, and as a leader God
calls you to shepherd the heart. You must be regularly
calling people to examine their actions, motives, desires,
and relationships to make course corrections. For example, you may hand out a list of probing verses, then lead
people in a time of reflection. Or you may address
thought patterns or behaviors prevalent in our society.
Generally speaking the heart is most convicted of sin
when it understands, not when it is categorically con-
demned. Don't blast people; instead help them see from
God's perspective so that they understand.

Speak for love. Shepherding knows no thing greater
than provoking members to love and good deeds. The eas-
iest place to do this is during activities that minister. When
you speak, urge members to respond to one another.
When they hear another pray for them, when someone
verbally tells another why they are a blessing to them,
when they hear another cry out to God on their behalf, it
strengthens the bonds of love. You can speak this way, and
you can lead them to speak this way to one another. For
example, before you pray for a member, you may say something like, "We are going to pray for Barbara Ann right
now. Barbara Ann, I want you to know how much you
mean to us. You have served faithfully in the children's program, you have been a blessing by your generosity, and
your desserts at fellowship dinners have made us all a little

fatter. I want you to know that we love you, and we're going to walk through this season of life with you."

Conclusion

As a shepherd you will guide people to walk with God, teaching them to live in relationship with him, getting on his agenda, and ministering to one another. You will do this by your lifestyle, attitude, the format and activities you choose, and the words you say. The words you say must be especially targeted to their hearts from the passion of your heart.

→ CHAPTER 7 ←

Discerning the
Activity of God

Recently a pastor of a small congregation told how praying in the Sunday morning service had revolutionized their church life. They went from a normal budget for a church start to receiving a $2.5 million building and a commitment of $1.7 million from an estate. Moreover, the church has grown significantly and continues to increase. Not surprisingly, this church's journey into corporate prayer coincided with a vision of the pastor to reach out to their community. Obviously, they connected; they discerned what God was up to in their church life and prayed accordingly.

Ultimately, this ability to know God's voice, to perceive his working, determines dynamic prayer. The format, activities, and shepherding assume this vital responsibility. No other ability even remotely rivals this one in importance. If we can't discern the activity of God, we cannot do anything else.

So how do you do that? How do you know the leading of God? When you plan the prayer meeting, how would you connect with God? This chapter divides that process into three categories: discerning God's activity before the prayer meeting, discerning God's activity during the prayer meeting, and discerning God's activity after prayer meeting.

Discerning God's Activity before the Prayer Meeting

Power with God flows from a God-centered, working relationship with God, and the primary purpose of prayer is a lifestyle of walking with God. That means you want a prayer meeting in line with God's activity. You will plan commensurate with what God has been doing, or you will plan in such a way that the church seeks to discover what he is doing. You will take three steps toward that end:

1. *Get alone with God.* Set aside undistracted time so that you will be able to pray and reflect. Go to a place where you won't be interrupted. Take a Bible with you, a pen, paper, and the format sheet to write down what you sense.

2. *Meditate on the activity of God.* Now you are ready to start reflecting on God's activity. Be ready to record what you sense. Once you know where God is leading your church or your small group, simply design your prayer meeting around that. But how do you meditate to identify the activity of God?

Growing up, I collected Indian artifacts as a hobby. Wherever Indians lived, people find buried relics of an ancient past recorded in stone, shell, bone, and pottery. Arrowheads, drills, scrapers, tomahawks, beads, gorgets, pottery, fishhooks, and assorted tools may be found if you know where to look. But therein lies the trick. How would you know where someone lived thousands of years ago with not one shred of visible evidence left to mark the spot? To search haphazardly would be much like looking for a diamond ring by randomly going to yard sales. When the possibilities are as vast as the whole country, just how does someone know where to start?

Discerning the activity of God carries similar analogies. Just how would you know where to start? What are the handles for filtering through the randomness of life so that we pinpoint where to look? Knowing where and how to look greatly increases the likelihood of perceiving God.

When I sought to identify where Indians lived in my region, I came to the table with three handles. First, I knew they always lived near running water. After all, who wants to carry water for miles or drink from a stagnant, mosquito-infested swamp? Second, they lived on ground above the flood plain; that's self-explanatory.

Third, the ground must have a good bit of level land. No one wants to live on a hill. They wanted enough space for several families to live there, and they needed ground for planting crops. This knowledge saved me much wasted effort, but I had one more tool to aid me even more. Instead of driving down roads to sight locate these sites, I used a topographical map (showing terrain elevation and water sources). I could identify these geographic features without ever setting foot outside my house.

Similarly, at least three arenas and one tool help us know where to look for God's activity. The arenas are his work among his people, your specific assignment, and impacting the world. The Bible serves as a tool. This record of his past actions and character serves as the spiritual equivalent of terrain elevation lines and water sources on the map, giving us a way to identify his activity in our lives. Knowing how to inspect these three arenas will guide how we plan and conduct a prayer meeting. Let's take each one of these individually.

God's work among his people. As Jesus faced imminent death, he prepared the disciples by letting them in on a secret so mind-boggling they couldn't even remotely understand him. He would indeed leave them, but in his place he would send another Helper. This particular Greek word for another in John 14:16 means "one that carries no difference whatsoever in kind or quality." This Helper, the Holy Spirit, would act with them in exactly the same way as Jesus had. That means one of the best ways to recognize the Holy Spirit's work with us is to study what Jesus did with his followers.

When you look at Jesus' work with the disciples in the Gospels, what do you see? Just as he gave assignments, trained, encouraged, rebuked, corrected, ministered to, built their faith, sent them out on mission trips, and opened their understanding, even so the Holy Spirit does that among the people of God today. When you want to identify God's activity, do the following:

- Pay attention to how your people's spiritual understanding is being affected.
- Listen to what they're learning in the Bible.
- Watch what starts surfacing in people's hearts related to serving or a biblical concern.
- Look for areas of growth in people's lives.
- Looks for areas of growth that are needed in their lives.
- Look for who is hurting or in a difficult situation needing ministry.
- Watch for opportunities for your members to discern God at work and to join him in it.
- Look for what has recently focused your church on God.
- Watch the testimonies that arise. Look for how God has worked and answered.
- What has come to your heart that bears sharing?

These clues will be vital to recognizing God's leading.

Your specific assignment. When you look at the activity of God in the life of Jesus, you see it connected to his assignment for Jesus. God didn't work through Jesus at random but rather expressed himself especially as it related to his purpose for his Son. For example, why was Jesus unknown until age thirty? Because the Spirit of God most likely did not do a public miracle through Jesus before then. When he came to his hometown, everybody was shocked at his wisdom and miraculous powers (Matt. 13:53–36). Apparently, this ordinary hometown boy had never done anything of note. But at the beginning of his earthly ministry, a significant event occurred. At his baptism the Spirit descended upon him. He then "returned in the power of the Spirit" teaching, performing miracles, and casting out demons. He preached the opening lines of his first hometown sermon by saying, "The Spirit of the Lord is upon Me because . . ." (Luke 4:18), and he listed six functions of what the Spirit's working through him would look like during his ministry. When Jesus was thirty, the Spirit began to work through him in ways related to his assignment as Messiah and Redeemer.

That means the activity of God will especially be connected to the arena of your assignment. Understanding his assignment kept Jesus walking in the Spirit. It determined his decision to go to other towns and villages (Mark 1:37), when to leave Judea (John 7:1), when to go back to Judea (John 11:7), when to perform mighty works, and when not to perform mighty works (Matt. 13:58). This principle also works for the saints of the Bible as well. Think of how God worked through Moses, Joshua, David, Paul, and Peter. The Spirit's working through them matched the fulfilling of their assignment. Similarly, when you know your assignment, then you know to look for an arena in which God will work. This assignment relates both to how you serve in the body of Christ and how your group or church is to reach out to the world around you. If God has given you an assignment to build up fatherless children in a housing project, constantly be looking to see what is happening in that arena. If he has called your group to cover your pastor in prayer, constantly be looking to see what the Spirit is doing in your pastor's life. Don't spend inordinate energy looking for God in a sphere that does not relate to your assignment, but expect to look for him according to the purpose he has given you. Here are five questions that may help you:

- What is our church/small group assignment?
- What needs to happen in order to fulfill our assignment?
- Do those in our assignment need ministry?
- What did we pray last? What did God do?
- Have any doors opened?

Impacting the world. The Spirit also worked through Jesus to impact those who were not his immediate followers. God desires to give all nations to his Son as an inheritance. The life of Paul affirms that the message of salvation is to be delivered to all, for God desires all to come to a saving knowledge of the truth (1 Tim. 2:4). Therefore, the Spirit will be drawing, contending with, and convicting the world. When you see God at work in people's lives, you should be praying for those people.

- Especially look for those with a seeking heart for spiritual things.
- Watch for opportunities that make hearts tender toward God.
- Watch for open doors, such as disaster relief opportunities after a storm, or a public school asking for help with latchkey kids, or a nursing home approaching you for help.
- What has your community been receptive to? For example, our church has knocked on the doors of our neighborhood without much success. Recently, an out-of-town minister knocked on doors in our neighborhood just to ask how he could pray for people. People responded very positively when he expressed a desire to pray for them instead of asking something from them.

Not every hoop means jump, but some will be of God. We are not saved by good works, but God has prepared good works for those who are saved (Eph. 2:8–10). These good works bless people and open the door to proclaim the gospel.

Meditate on God's activity by reflecting on each one of these arenas. Consider whether scriptural insights and/or circumstances might mesh.

Scripture. If you begin understanding a passage or have a quickening in your spirit from it, stop and ask God why he is bringing this to your attention. Then meditate on how it applies to the three arenas and three desires of God. Write down what you sense.

Circumstances. What challenges is the church facing? What opportunities have arisen? What have we been asking and what has happened in the last seven days? Do I see a pattern that fits the pattern of God's working in Scripture? Write down what you sense.

	His Work among His People	Assignment	Impacting the World
Scripture and Circumstances			

3. *Design the prayer meeting.* On your paper you should have identified insights from Scripture and circumstances as they relate to God's work among his people, your assignment, and ways of impacting the world. Simply transfer this to the appropriate blanks on the format sheet.

Discerning and Responding during the Prayer Meeting

Wherever two or three are gathered in Jesus' name, he is in the midst of them. The Holy Spirit is the leader of the prayer meeting, not a person. As an undershepherd your number one assignment is to please him. At times the meeting may go exactly as planned. At other times the Holy Spirit will do something unexpected that may require change in the original plans. In order to walk with God, you must do two things.

First, you must identify the working of God in the prayer meeting. Have you ever wondered how you would know if this were God? What would his working look like? What's the difference between emotionalism and his working? How will I know when God is answering us? When people share something on their hearts, is it from them or from God? This understanding is critical.

Second, when you see God moving, you must know how to respond. When would you change your plans or keep doing what you have been doing? What would you change your plans to?

1. *Work with God by identifying his work in the prayer meeting.* God's work especially revolves around his three desires of revealing himself to his people, moving them onto his agenda, and ministering to them. You will best identify this in the prayer meeting if you pay attention in two ways.

First, observe the faces and behavior of your people. Here are some ways to do that:

- Watch people's faces as you or others talk.
- Look for eye contact.
- Watch body language.
- Watch how people are interacting with one another.
- Regularly keep your eyes open during prayer time.

- During small group prayer times, eavesdrop on what different groups are praying.
- Pray in a small group yourself.

You may not do every one of these every time, but you get the idea. Put yourself in a position to read people's hearts through their faces and behavior.

Second, look for evidences of the Spirit's working. Pay attention to fervency, understanding, personal growth, the cry of the heart, focusing, and building unity. Here are some examples of what to look for in the Spirit's working:

- *Increasing intensity of the prayers.* When the prayer meeting becomes more animated, often God is speaking to hearts.
- *Touching hearts.* When eyes are wet, that's often a clue.
- *Crying out.* Some people have a heart burden so strong that they will cry out. One time in prayer meeting, a man deeply burdened interrupted the prayer meeting to request prayer for his church about to go through a split. It turned out several others were in that same situation. We prayed for those churches, and it powerfully ministered to them.
- *Conviction of sin.* When people fall under conviction, you clearly know God is at work. Only the Spirit of God will cause a person to face his sin. John Avant, a pastor, tells how the Spirit of God fell in his church unexpectedly one

morning. A college student shared a word from God, and immediately people were cut to the heart. So great was God's moving that they did not have the normal worship service; rather, they continued the whole time in prayer and confession of sin.

- *People gaining insight while praying.* Recently my wife and I were praying over a delicate situation that needed God's intervention. As we prayed, an insight came to her mind. She prayed it out loud, and it set my thinking in the same direction but also triggered more insight. We came to have wisdom regarding the subject at hand. Often in prayer God will guide by touching the understanding of those praying. In fact, sometimes the group may start by praying in one direction but end up praying in another. Many times this will be accompanied by insight into Scripture. This is a clue that God may be speaking. I have found this type of God's working to happen especially among people who have a common heart burden.

- *Watching for what comes to mind while you pray.* This is much like gaining insight but with a difference. Sometimes no insight is present, but someone comes to mind, and you have a burden or a sense that he or she needs a touch from the Lord. Last year in our prayer meeting, one of our godly members began praying for another church member. Unbeknownst to any of us, this lady had just given up her job because doing what was being asked of her would have violated her integrity. Understandably she came to prayer meeting that night with a heavy heart seeking God. She was ministered to, and before the next prayer meeting, God had given her another job with better pay and hours.

- *Refocusing*. Many times we begin praying from a self-orientation and end up praying from a biblical orientation. I learned this in the first prayer group I ever participated in. On several occasions we would begin praying for a request the way we thought would be best but end up praying from more of a kingdom perspective by the time the prayer ended. Typically this happened by the process of praying Scripture and meditation.

- *Building unity*. Building unity is a major assignment for the Spirit of God. When members become burdened for one another, we should always pay attention. In my home church a member mentioned wanting to do something one night for another member who needed God's touch. This included sending a birthday card, but she mentioned she had been unable to prepare it ahead of time. I encouraged her to leave the prayer meeting and make the card while we were praying. We were able to minister to him at the end of the meeting by signing the card and giving money. In Romans 14:20 Paul commanded the people not to destroy the "work of God" over theological differences regarding food. He recognized the work of God was building or maintaining the unity of the Spirit. When you see members ministering to one another and the body being built up, that's the work of God.

- *Coming into agreement.* Members may begin by praying in different directions. When their prayers become unified so that everyone is of one heart and mind, that's just like what the Spirit did in the book of Acts.
- *Orienting people.* You can see when people move from distraction to rapt attention. That's often a clue that God is leading in a certain direction.
- *Using testimonies.* Testimonies often excite people to prayer or instruct them in how to pray. Watch how people respond to a testimony, and you may get a clue to God's activity. God sometimes does something for one member during the week because he wants to speak to the church. The testimony may be a message from the Lord to the church body for a certain direction, or it may be an encouragement toward genuine prayer.
- *People receiving the same spiritual message or similar experiences.* Watch for patterns when people share what God has been saying. Recently in

our church prayer meeting, a member interrupted and asked if he could tell everyone what
God had been saying to him. Of course, everyone agreed. One member shared that God had
been drawing him closer. That triggered
another member to share that God had been
leading her to read the Bible instead of the
paper in the morning. Another shared that God
had said the same basic thing to him. The following week a fourth member shared how God
had been speaking to refocus him also. When
members have similar experiences with the same
spiritual message, usually God is in this.

- *People being ministered to.* Ephesians 4:16 says the
  body builds itself up in love as each member
  does its part. In 1 Corinthians 12 Paul explains
  that actually the Spirit of God is the one working through each member. When the people of
  God begin to be built up, you are seeing his
  hand. One time I saw this modeled was when a
  leader led people to bless one another in the
  name of the Lord. He orchestrated a time to let
  participants publicly tell why they thanked God
  for them. Those hearing and giving words of
  affirmation were powerfully built up in a way
  that I have rarely seen excelled.

- *Conforming to Christ's image.* Some of God's
  working requires no immediate response, but as
  a shepherd you need to file it away for future

reference. Watch for growth in the lives of participants. Who is praying out loud for the first time? Who is now ready to give a testimony? Who is ready to step up to a leadership role? You may be ready to capitalize on this. About a year after 9/11 I heard Jim Cymbala, a pastor from New York City, speak at a conference. Before he preached, a woman with him gave a testimony. She was the last one pulled out alive from the rubble. As a shepherd he gave her a platform to glorify God through her story. He guided her in walking with God, and he recognized her witness would powerfully impact the body of Christ. He capitalized on an opportunity for conforming her and others into the image of Christ.

2. *Work with God by responding with sensitivity to his work among the people.* When God begins to move, how should you respond? How will you know whether to cancel your plans or continue with your format? How would you fan and not quench the working of the Spirit? If you were to make adjustments, what would you do? Below are some questions with examples of how to respond.

- How will you know when to make changes? Your changes should follow these principles.
  (1) You change when God begins working in a way that is different from what you had planned. This may occur as an interruption or

as a growing awareness that people's hearts are leaning another direction. (2) If you do make changes, they need to be in line with what is already obviously happening. If you are unclear whether God is at work, continue as you have been. (3) If what God is accomplishing in hearts requires more time, increase or change a prayer time if you sense people are still being ministered to, or a truth is sinking in, or dealing with sin is not yet complete. Occasionally an entire format may be changed. Many times it's a subtle tweak to one particular section. Do not try to determine changes based on emotions but on what God is accomplishing. You do not necessarily need to change just because you recognize God's working. Sometimes a prayer meeting will be animated with a sense of God's presence, but you will continue through the format as planned. The rule that guides your decision will be discerning whether everyone is in step with God.

- How will you get back on your format? There are two answers to this. (1) If it's just a small detour, get back on where you got off. Or you may drop a segment of the prayer time that you had planned. (2) You may not need to get back to your format.
- What would you do if you had to nix someone you had lined up to do something? Set expecta-

tions ahead of time. Tell that person if God moves we will change what we had planned.

- When do you move on to the next prayer time? When people are praying in pairs or small groups, typically I watch for half or two-thirds of the people to finish. Then I prompt the instrumentalist to begin playing soft, instrumental music. This cues the people that it's time to wrap things up.

- What do you do if someone breaks down? You may do one of several things. Stop and pray for him or her right then. Have another to come pray with the individual. If the person is terribly upset, you may want to have someone gently escort him or her out to pray together in another room.

- What do you do if someone begins confessing sin? Always be ready to step in. Sin can be confessed appropriately or inappropriately. For example, inappropriate public confession would be naming names of whom one has sinned with, shifting or excusing personal sin, or telling lurid details. You always need to be ready to step in and say something like, "Obviously, brother, you are experiencing grief over this. I'd like to ask a couple of deacons to go with you where they can more fully respond to the concerns of your heart." If it's a woman, ask two ladies to go with her. Ask two because some confessions are of such a nature that it's better for there to be two witnesses.

- How do you respond when someone expresses a burden? In a large group there will typically be others experiencing the same thing. Usually it's good to ask if someone else has the same burden and then pray for everyone in that group. When it's time to pray, move people to minister to one another.

Discerning God's Activity after the Prayer Meeting

Once we ask, God will answer. We need to watch to see what that answer is. Recognizing how God answered will inform us how to pray next. It may also impact how we plan the next prayer meeting. There will be much overlap between this section and planning for a prayer meeting; therefore this section will be short. There are three comments of note, however.

1. *Look for answers to prayer.* Once we pray, we must look for how God responds. Too many times we forget what we prayed, or we don't really expect an answer. Instead, we must constantly have our radar on to identify God's answers.

2. *Recognize God's answers.* Connecting the dots between what we asked and how God responds is often a challenge. When we pray earnestly, God always answers,

although that answer may take on a number of forms. Here are some examples of the ways God may answer.

- God gives insight. In the Gospels Jesus almost never answered the disciples with a yes, and he almost never answered them with a no. He usually answered them in such a way that they came to understand his person and his purpose better. This confused the disciples greatly. His answers puzzled them because they could not grasp what he meant. By the book of Acts, however, they usually understood. Generally when Jesus answered this way, it was because he was trying to correct their praying. For example, James and John wanted to call fire down from heaven. Jesus did not answer with a flat no; he answered that they didn't understand his purpose. He came to save men's lives, not to kill them. He was correcting their prayer through giving them insight. Sometimes God will answer a church, but the church misses God because they merely seek to gauge an answer by whether God did what they asked. Other times they may have a sense of confusion. The confusion is not bad if they continue to pray through until they understand.

- God works but in a different direction from what we expected. The disciples kept wondering when Jesus would restore the kingdom. He told them not to worry about it; the Holy Spirit was coming, and they would be his witnesses. They wanted to sit on the right and the left; he taught humility. Mary and Martha wanted Jesus to keep their brother from dying. Jesus answered by allowing death and announcing it was for the glory of God. It is hard to receive an answer from God when it doesn't match our expectations. Sometimes we pray in one direction, but God answers us by trying to move us into another. Too many times we say God didn't answer our prayer. Sometimes we pray for healing of someone dear. When God heals that person, it is easy. When he doesn't, we must look to see what else he has in mind.

- A door of opportunity opens. Sometimes we pray and God does something not even on our radar screen. Ananias had no inkling that Paul had been converted and had seen in a vision that someone would lay hands on him to receive his sight. Peter had no clue about Cornelius. Paul and Silas didn't know an earthquake was coming that would result in the conversion of the Philippian jailer. One of the best prayers to pray is, "God, I am your servant. What is your will?" then watch to see what happens. He may open a door for a church to serve him in an area they hadn't considered before.

- God is silent. Often we can't discern any response after praying. In those cases we need to continue to pray and watch. Sometimes the silence of God is to prepare us for something important. For example, in Revelation 8:1, when the seventh seal was opened, a half hour of silence followed. That ominous stillness added gravity to the seven trumpet blasts that were to follow. Other times silence comes because of sin in our lives. In that case God intends his silence to communicate that something is wrong in our relationship with him, leading us to introspection. Other times silence encourages personal growth, driving us more deeply to search out the things of God. In all three instances silence is an answer that should impact our response.

- He does what we ask.
- God says no.

3. *Follow up.* As a shepherd there will be times when you need to get involved in others' lives based on what you see in the prayer meeting. If someone continually requests prayer about a self-inflicted crisis, you may want to meet with that person to help him or her overcome such destructive personal patterns. If someone has a tremendous burden, what happens that week may have tremendous impact in his or her walk with God. You may take initiative to help people interpret how to respond based on what God does or does not do. If God is working in someone's life in an unusual way, God may want to set his life in a direction he hadn't considered. As a shepherd you may need to help guide him in the process of discovering what God is saying. If a couple announces

their engagement, you want to help them get resources for this significant time in their life. Pray about how God wants you to respond in the week based on what you see in the prayer meeting.

Conclusion

Discerning God's activity will be the foundation for guiding prayer. Understanding him will radically impact what we plan to request of him. Seek to understand him at all times—before, during, and after the prayer meeting. Pay special attention to any opportunities for shepherding based on what you discern in prayer meeting.

CHAPTER 8

Making the Transition

Introduction

Recently I talked with a pastor of a church where revival had broken out. They had scheduled revival services, and it actually happened. God began moving in a powerful way. Members experienced a dramatic renewal in their relationship with God; the lost were converted; meetings ran long, and no one complained. One of the humorous stories that illustrate God's working happened with an elderly member. Her family called her home repeatedly one Friday night, but she didn't answer the phone. Fearing the worst, they drove to her house at midnight, only to discover she was still at church! The spirit of revival has infused their prayer meetings with a deep richness, a fervency, a sense of communion with God. Because of the joy they have in the presence of God, they no longer watch the clock, and they are seeing him move in many exciting ways. Is that not what we all want?

The previous chapters have argued a case for corporate prayer, explained the mixture of key foundations and responsibilities, and given practical ideas for leading. But one hurdle remains for the majority who will pick up this book. You could do all the "right" things but still lack any authentic life in prayer meeting. Some catalytic event must occur; a defining moment must trigger a change; a radical paradigm shift must materialize; or you will merely rearrange the sand in the hourglass. That leap from A to B is called *transition*. The people must move from stale practices of status quo to vibrantly encountering the presence of God. You must successfully navigate the dangerous shoals of undoing old thought patterns and habits to establish new ones. This will prove to be one of your greatest tests of leadership. Rarely will a leader face a greater challenge than charting a course through transition. Few things will stretch you more than the dual requirement of reversing the old and instituting the new. I recommend that the transition consist of at least four main actions: prepare, involve, transition, and reinforce.

Prepare Hearts

It's wise to begin the same way God does. When he sought to move his people in a new direction, how did he do it? No clearer example rises from the pages of Scripture than the ministry of Jesus. God was about to transition from the Old Covenant to the New, from being under law to grace, from an earthly priesthood to a heavenly one. Luke 3 records the launching of this cataclysmic earthquake that would rock the spiritual face of world history. Watch how he does it. First, he preceded the revelation of his Son by sending John the Baptist. Luke 3:4 states that the purpose of John was to "prepare the way of the Lord." That immediately raises these questions: "Why would Jesus need John to prepare the way? Was he not good enough? Couldn't he have done it himself? And being the Son of God, couldn't he have done a better job?"

The text proves even more odd upon studying it a little more closely. God chose to send Jesus at a time of extreme wickedness and oppressive leadership. Consider what it would have been like to have lived under the reign of Annas, Caiaphas, and Herod, as well as being dominated by Rome under Caesar and Pilate. On top of that God had not spoken for four hundred years. Just imagine the magnitude of that time span. If you were to subtract four hundred years off American history, what would you have? What was God doing? Why in the world would he send his Messiah into these circumstances?

We solve the riddle by reading the results it worked in the people. Four centuries of silence and nearly a hundred years of Roman occupation served to pique their readiness for change. When God unexpectedly exploded his plan, every head snapped around in rapt attention. The people who walked in darkness suddenly saw a great light. John's ministry rumbled like thunder, foreshadowing an imminent deluge upon a drought-stricken land. What would people naturally have begun talking about? Can you imagine the topic of conversation in the synagogues, the marketplace, and the supper table that followed? Luke 3:15 records precisely what it was: "Now as the people were in expectation, and all reasoned in their hearts about John, whether he was the Christ or not." Do you see what God was doing? They began asking about a Messiah—the exact question God wanted to answer. He caused them to thirst for the water he was about to give. The appearance of John was the trumpet blast preparing their hearts for the direction God was moving.

This pattern of preparation harmonizes with other biblical stories. When God decided to choose a people for himself, why didn't he just destroy the Egyptians at once? Why did he deliver the children of Israel through a series of ten plagues? You can see those judgments, favoring the Hebrews over the Egyptians, prepared Moses and the children of Israel for heart change. The crescendo effect of God's intervention began to transform their faith. Moses went from timidity in plague one to superabundant boldness by plague ten. Numbers 33:3 and Exodus 14:8 record that the beaten-down, subjugated, nobody slaves marched out of Egypt boldly in the face of their oppressors. In David's case, when God sought to change kings, why did he delay over twenty years from the time of David's anointing until he placed him on the throne of Israel? When David killed Goliath, endured the unjust persecution of Saul, and renounced the murder of Abner, it leavened the heart understanding of the Israelites to recognize God's activity. In 1 Chronicles 12:38 the people came to Jerusalem with one mind to make David king. The circumstances and processes prepared them to transition from one kingdom to the next.

Since God preceded each new direction with preparation, that tells us the people of God are not inherently wired to respond immediately to God the moment he begins moving. He first readies their minds and hearts. The same will be true of your prayer meeting. The soil must first be cleared of stones, the heart roots dug out, and the soil tilled before seeking to implement anything. God will be the primary one doing this. He will be working in hearts, arranging circumstances, and putting everything in place. But you must work with him in that process. Moses, David, John the Baptist, and Jesus didn't sip lemonade and play checkers. They testified what God's will was and did everything toward that end to further the kingdom. You likewise have that responsibility.

You will do this for a season by implementing these four steps.

1. *Model and teach.* Would it not be unfair to expect someone to function well in China who has never been taught Chinese? In the same way, if the majority in your group or church has never or rarely tasted the sweetness of God's presence in prayer meeting, then how would they know what to do? When you speak of being God-centered, entering his presence, or discerning his activity, is it reasonable to expect them to know how to respond? Would it not make sense that they must first be equipped with the understanding of how to relate to God? Failure to break up the fallow ground will make for a rough planting season. You will do this by changing neither format nor activities initially. Rather, you will model and teach. Let them grapple with Scripture. Let them hear testimonies. Let their eyes acclimate to the light of what could be. God will use these truths over time to prepare them for a different pattern of relating to him.

When you model and teach, especially highlight God-centeredness, worship, love for God, faith, and desire. Guide your people to enter his presence with thanksgiving in their hearts and his courts with praise. Redirect them from merely praying for needs to seeking the person of God. Model how to practice confidence in God. Let them see your genuine love for the Lord. Create opportunities for other members with a like heart and wonderful testimonies to share. These practices will begin to set a standard for different expectations.

2. *Change the mentality.* In modeling and teaching a different pattern, you will do two things that threaten some people, especially those steeped in traditionalism. You will be challenging the practices that they're accustomed to and the beliefs they have about the purpose of prayer. I've asked five thousands leaders over the last five years this question: *When was the last time you remember the manifest presence and power of God on a regular basis in your midweek prayer meeting?* The majority remains silent, but usually a few will answer. When they do, their response generally has fallen into two categories. Either they say recently, or they say it was in 1954. I believe God is stirring us right now, and that explains why some answer recently.

If the last time God moved mightily on a regular basis in your midweek prayer meetings was in the 1950s, you are at least sixty years old. That means most Americans living today have not experienced a dynamic prayer meeting. In its place we've practiced a service we call prayer meeting, but the pattern we've modeled is to take requests and pray for them. No one I know has ever verbally taught that the primary purpose of prayer is to meet needs, but actions speak louder than words. We've communicated that God created prayer preeminently to take care of requests rather than to have a relationship and seek the kingdom. Through modeling and teaching, God must transform the mentality of your people regarding prayer. This groundwork prepares them to think, expect, and act differently.

3. *Pray for a reference point for dynamic prayer.* A few
years ago I sat with a group of denominational prayer
leaders asking questions of the staff at the Brooklyn
Tabernacle, a dynamic praying church. Someone asked,
"What causes people to seek the face of God in prayer so
that they don't pray for just a few shallow minutes?" The
answer given followed along these lines: "They need to
have an experience with God in prayer where they
encounter him for an extended time. Once people
encounter him, it alters their reference point. From then
on they know by experience the difference, and it makes
them dissatisfied with anything less." In a typical church
most people will not have this reference point, so they
don't intuitively know how to function. Hearing the
word of God and dynamic testimonies can create a
yearning for what could be, but encountering the presence of God turns understanding the possibility into
understanding the reality. From then on they can discern
between status quo and dynamism. Obviously you cannot manufacture the presence of God, but you can ask
him to reveal himself. Your responsibility is to be faithful as you wait on him.

4. *Challenge traditionalism.* Mentalities, old practices,
and experiences create tradition. Never should we view
tradition as bad, for God himself instituted traditions.
He intended them to be a powerful communicator of
truth, evoking resolve for following him. For example,
if you are a Christian, what does the Lord's Supper stir
in you? The familiarity with the ritual instantly calls to

heart all your years of understanding the cross, renewing and strengthening your faith. No, tradition is not bad; however, *traditionalism* is. When rituals turn stale, are misapplied or misunderstood, their inherent power for good morphs into an intractable leech on spiritual vibrancy. Unfortunately, practicing a prayer meeting for decades without the presence of God has bequeathed us practices and beliefs that substitute for God. You must challenge these. The best way to soften these leftover forms of godliness for removal is with the oil of teaching, testimonies, modeling, and involving others.

Involve Others

If you want people to walk with God, lead people to be involved in that walk. If you are a lone ranger, making all decisions solely by yourself, don't be surprised when no one responds to those unilateral decisions. The process must lead the people to walk together with each playing a different role. The Israelites began their transition from camping at Mount Sinai for a year to marching on the promised land. They did not break camp by just grabbing up their belongings and marching off. Instead each person moved in an orderly fashion, organized around the ark and the tabernacle. The priests and Levites served a particular function, and the tribes marched out in ranks following each one's respective standard. This organization, orchestration, and procession served more than just a functional purpose.

Involving each Israelite imparted a sense of togetherness and mission, girding up the loins of their minds for action (see Num. 10).

Consider these three things to involve others:

1. *Begin with leadership.* If your church leaders have no heart for changes in a prayer meeting, you can be confident that few others will either. When your leaders gain a heart for God, then others will gain that same heart. When they become convinced that your church must become a praying church, they will exhort others in that same direction.

2. *Consider small groups for informal mentoring.* What if no one has a heart for praying? You should consider backing off changing the structure of the prayer meeting and take a different angle. You may want to ask three or four of your leaders to join you for a weekly prayer time. An invitation could be something as simple as, "I've been wanting to go deeper with God. Have you had that desire too? I'm asking you and two others if we can meet once a week (or every two weeks, or once a month) for the next three months to seek the face of God. We're going to be studying about prayer and then put that teaching into practice. We're also going to make a list and keep a record of what God does."

When God begins answering, this will create a different set of expectations and understanding of how to walk with God in prayer. Your leaders will carry that excitement into prayer meeting, and their enthusiasm will begin to influence others. This may take some time.

You may cycle through three or four groups before God has changed people enough to institute changes to the prayer meeting.

3. *Get feedback.* You need to know the response level of your people and whether God is opening their understanding. You should ask questions of the people and especially receive feedback from your leaders. This feedback grants handles for knowing how God is working in your people.

Transition the Prayer Meeting

How do you transition practically? How would you change the format and integrate activities? First, know the balance in your relational bank account with the people. If you have gained their trust by loving them and if you have a track record of successful changes, you will find receptivity to change in prayer meetings. If you have had strained relations with members in the past, that lack of relationship will affect their level of willingness to follow. If you have written "bad checks" in past relations or are still overdrawn, consider whether you ought to be more concerned with changing a format and activities prior to repair work. If you are new, consider how you can build good relationships before making changes or how you can do both simultaneously.

1. *Implement by integration.* Radically, immediately changing format and activities in most churches creates trouble. I've met a number of pastors whose people quit

coming when they changed their prayer meeting all at once. The lack of reference point proved so uncomfortable that they extricated themselves from attending. People usually change in a series of small steps. You may have to exercise great patience as God works in hearts. Remember, your ultimate goal is not to transform a prayer meeting but to transform a people. Don't begin by dismantling everything you are already doing. Capitalize on what you already do. Below are suggestions for integrating the five segments of the format from a typical midweek prayer meeting that has the four elements of singing, teaching/preaching, taking requests, and praying for them.

Focus on God. Convert the singing/teaching/preaching time into this segment. You can begin teaching on prayer, the attributes of God, or what the Bible says God likes. You may consider a series of messages. Do not worry about the length of time. Let it stay the same initially. In fact, in teaching how to relate to God and to recognize God's working, the longer time will be to your advantage.

Respond from the heart. After preaching or teaching the Word, ask questions for personal application. You may say something as simple as, "Before we take requests, let's pause a moment and ask God to speak to us about what we've just heard," or, "Based on the Scripture we've just heard, how did you see God work this week?" or, "Has anything in your heart changed over the past four weeks? Did you recognize that change as God?" Then allow for a time of response in silence or praying in small groups. Integrate this with your teaching time from the Focus on God segment.

Seek first the kingdom. After a few weeks you may say, "I want us to do something different tonight. We've been studying about the Lord's Prayer the past ten weeks, and he told us to seek first the kingdom. Let's do just that. We have a mission team leaving next week, and we're going to pray for them." A great follow-up in this example would be to have the team report after their trip and pray again. Add this segment after establishing a response time.

Present your requests. You probably will already be practicing taking requests, but you may redirect the focus and structure of the time to be God-centered. Let this follow the focus on God (preaching/teaching) and response time. See chapter 5 for ideas on activities.

Close in celebration. You already have some way to close services. You will be giving it an attitude of celebrating God's goodness.

This suggested way of transitioning assumes the passing of time so that God may work in hearts. In certain cases it may be possible to change the format all at once. You could do that in one of two ways. First, announce a focused time of six weeks. Highlight each segment and teach on it, then practice it that evening. Six weeks will allow you to comment on each one and put them all into practice together. This will create understanding and allow enough time for people to become used to it.

2. *Establish the format and core activities.* In chapter 5 I gave numerous suggested activities for two reasons. First, you have the option of choosing one you like. Second, this variety gives you fresh ideas so that you don't fall in a rut. However, creativity is not a stand-alone virtue. Doing something different for its own sake may do more harm than good. Most people function best when they become familiar with a pattern. Routine frees people to focus in prayer rather than to try to concentrate on something new. It's much like learning new music. It's hard to worship God through it when you're trying to learn the words and the tune. Similarly, when people become familiar with a set of activities, they can concentrate on God more easily. Therefore, you ought to establish a pattern for your prayer meeting.

I'm suggesting five core elements that ought to be a staple of your prayer meeting. The ones selected are based on my experience, others' experience, or gleaning from history what God has especially used:

Format. You can use the one I've suggested or change it, but you will want to establish a regular pattern.

Bible. Prayer meetings will languish without the Word of God renewing our hearts and guiding our prayers.

Testimonies. These greatly stir the heart and remind the people of what God can do. Hearing about God's work builds faith and increases desire.

Vocal prayer in small groups. Small groups lend themselves to involvement, relationship building, and being in one accord. If I were stripped to only one participation activity, it would be this one. (Some churches prefer praying out loud all at once individually or in small groups.)

Ministering activities. This pleases God and draws people closer to one another. In my experience, when people pray for one another or show their love for one another, God blesses prayer meeting more than when practicing any other activity.

3. *Be prepared for challenges.* It would be impossible to list all the unforeseen challenges you will face, but you can be absolutely certain you will have some. I've listed some that have been common.

Fear of praying out loud. A number of your people may be afraid to pray aloud, which will negatively impact praying in small groups or pairs. Various reasons exist for this fear. Sometimes people lose sight that prayer is an expression of the heart to God; instead they worry about how others will perceive their performance. Some people prefer to be private and simply don't want others to hear their inner thoughts. Some favor passivity to participating. I've even heard the occasional objection that Satan will know how to circumvent our prayers if he hears what we ask (which has no biblical basis). Perhaps other reasons exist, but you will likely encounter this among a number of people in groups of any size.

What can you do? Precede change by teaching. Tell people why we must pray together and out loud. Point out that God uses his whole body, and others need to hear them. Further educate them that almost all prayer in the Bible was vocal. Occasionally you can see silent prayer in exceptional circumstances such as Hannah outside the door of the tabernacle or Nehemiah before the king, but most prayer was out loud. You may note how many times the phrase "cried out" occurs in Scripture, show various examples of others praying aloud, and show that even meditation in the Bible involved the voice (two examples of this are Joshua 1:8 and Psalm 5:1–3).

You may further help people by: (1) Having them pray one word or one sentence out loud. For example, you may lead an exercise where you ask people to call out the name of a lost person before God. Or you may have them name one thing for which they are grateful. They can do that in a simple sentence such as, "Father, I thank you for _____." Often taking a first step pushes them over the hump. (2) Break into small groups. People are less intimidated with friends in a small group than they are in a large group. (3) Finally, you may make allowance for people afraid to pray aloud by breaking people into small groups of six or more. This small group size is large enough that if they don't pray they won't feel singled out as much.

Lack of participation. Some people may be unfamiliar with a service requiring something from them. Others enjoy coasting in spectator mode. Still others just don't like change. Here are some ways to involve people.

- Enlist personally. Start with those who are most open. Ask them before prayer meeting to have a part. That may mean leading a prayer time for the whole group, giving a testimony, or sharing a request from the front. By modeling you will visibly show that others than the leader are playing a role in the prayer meeting.

- Highlight different groups to pray for. People rarely mind when a fellow church member fervently pleads for God's blessing upon them. The receptivity to prayer creates an opportunity to have a group of seniors, newlyweds, a mission team, or high schoolers to stand up to be prayed for. This requires participation from those being prayed for, and you can find ways to let those around them pray for them. For example, you may have two fathers and two mothers pray for the high schoolers. You may have the couple who has been married the longest pray for the newlyweds. You may let those who have been impacted by the seniors in the church stand beside them while someone leads a prayer.

- Select committees to report. You may select one or two committees each week to report on their work. Then you will ask someone to pray for them. This idea models and encourages participation—not to mention seeking the blessing of God.

Leading without manipulating or trying to create an effect. Sometimes as leaders we zealously desire our people to experience what we have experienced. When things don't happen fast enough for us, a temptation arises to manufacture that experience with God by using emotionalism or behavior modifications. However, emotions do not lead to an encounter with God; they are expressed as a by-product of it. Obedience will require behavior modifications, but merely acting a certain way does not produce the power of God. Instead we must target the understanding of the heart. When people respond to God because their minds have comprehended, they will act volitionally from their own desire. We must be patient and not succumb to manipulating prayer by fleshly efforts.

Maintaining a personal walk. Proverbs 4:23 admonishes us to *diligently* guard our heart. Our faith, fervency, and passion naturally wane under the relentless assault of life circumstances and demands. They must be renewed daily. Failure to do so renders us ineffective as spiritual leaders. We must not let the little foxes spoil the vines.

Reinforce

Jesus said, "Come after Me, and I will make you become . . ." (Mark 1:17). He transformed that lowly group from a hodgepodge band of insignificant followers into world changers. He moved them from consistent failure in the Gospels to consistently walking with God in Acts. When we look into Matthew, Mark, Luke, and John, we see a three-and-a-half-year transition period of the disciples, moving them from ordinary to elite. Jesus' main work involved transforming them to become. He did not hang his ministry upon modifying their behavior; rather, he hung his ministry upon changing them from the inside out. Here are some of the things he did.

1. *Repeat.* Jesus repeated himself a lot. He spoke of humility and faith over and over again. Luke scatters the Sermon on the Mount throughout his Gospel, which means Jesus probably taught it repeatedly in various settings. When you lead, you will do and say many of the same things over and over again. Even if people have heard it, tell them again. Constantly remind them of what they already know. You may teach certain catchphrases, remind members of key verses of Scripture, or restate the obvious. Make it interesting, but never underestimate how long it takes for words to sink down into someone's soul.

2. *Recognize.* When you see someone responding to God, going deeper with him, or God answering his prayer, highlight the activity of God in his life. Find ways to exalt God through giving these people opportunities to testify, assuming leadership roles appropriate for them, and verbally commending their obedience to others. Set visible standards for what those whom you lead should expect and become.

3. *Require accountability.* Jesus constantly required accountability. He asked his disciples where their faith was. He placed small children in their midst to teach humility. A church or small group must always remember what the standard is. Jesus set and held a standard. That accountability did not relate to behavior as much as to

whom his disciples were becoming. Jesus refused to let them be less than what God intended. Similarly, anything less than becoming like God should be viewed as unacceptable. The leader must not let friendship or intimidation result in softening the requirements or seeing God move powerfully.

The ultimate test for becoming is answering this question: "How is God responding to our prayers?" If God has not shown his favor on the church or small group, those praying ought to ask the question, "Why?" As a leader you must never let the standard for evaluating the prayer meeting be a method, a manner, eloquence, quantity, or format, but what God is affirming. If we are becoming who God made us, he will demonstrate his power on our behalf.

Conclusion

In this chapter we have reviewed issues related to making a transition. Of the things listed, the heart preparation and involvement will be the most important. God sets the pace. Watching for his working in hearts will guide you when to push or wait. Involving others impacts a passion for walking with God. The actual transition process of implementation may vary in your case. Reinforcing learning, becoming, and behavior will be especially true in the beginning but will continue throughout your tenure as a leader.

In this book we have seen the preponderance of evidence demanding that we pray together, the foundations for dynamic corporate prayer, the three desires of God and the four responsibilities a leader must execute to work with him, a suggested format, a host of activities to choose from, the requirement of shepherding, pointers for discerning God's activity, and keys for making a transition. Of all these the two most important responsibilities you can execute are personally discerning God's activity and shepherding your people to be God-centered.

Now for a final word from my heart. We desperately need revival. Prayer is not the last step before revival; repentance is. However, we will not repent if we are not in a position to hear God. That's one of the critical functions of corporate prayer. It will place two or more in that position. Then God's voice will be heard. Then hearts will respond. Then tears will fall. Then we will fall down trembling together at the voice of the Holy One speaking of sin and the judgment to come. Our broken souls lying prostrate before the Almighty will be raised to stand in the gap for this generation. May you, and thousands more like you, be the ones. Though I wrote generically on leadership principles for guiding others to pray together, my ultimate desire is that God may use this book toward this end.

May God bless you. "Now to Him who is able to do exceedingly abundantly above all that we ask or think, according to the power that works in us, to Him be glory in the church by Christ Jesus through all generations, world without end. Amen" (Eph. 3:20–21).

Jesus' Teaching on Prayer

The Criteria I used to Evaluate Jesus' Teaching on Prayer

1. I used the NKJV concordance and looked up the words *pray, prays, prayed, praying, prayer, prayers, ask, asks, asked asking, watch, watches, watched, watching.*

2. I counted verses (not words).

3. I counted those verses in which Jesus gave instruction about what to pray for or how to pray, and verses in which a command or a condition was required for a favorable answer to prayer.

4. I did not double-count a verse if two words appeared in the same verse (for example, if the verse says "Watch and pray . . ." I only counted it once).

5. I counted those verses that I deemed were commands that transcended a specific situation—commands that apply to us today.

6. I counted the duplicated verses of the Synoptic Gospels.

The Words I Searched and Their Verses

Verses in which the *you* was singular:

> Matthew 6:5–6,
>
> Matthew 7:8
>
> Luke 11:10

Verses in which the *you* was corporate:

> Matthew 5:44
>
> Matthew 6:7
>
> Matthew 6:8
>
> Matthew 6:9
>
> Matthew 7:7
>
> Matthew 7:8
>
> Matthew 9:38
>
> Matthew 17:21
>
> Matthew 18:19
>
> Matthew 21:22

Matthew 24:20
Matthew 24:42
Matthew 25:13
Matthew 26:41
Mark 9:29
Mark 11:24
Mark 11:25
Mark 13:18
Mark 13:33
Mark 13:35
Mark 13:37
Mark 14:38
Luke 6:28
Luke 10:2
Luke 11:2
Luke 11:9
Luke 11:10
Luke 18:1
Luke 21:36
John 14:13
John 14:14
John 15:7
John 15:16
John 16:23
John 16:24
John 16:26